WORKBOOK

M000025743

WORLD PASS

Expanding English Fluency

Susan Stempleski
Nancy Douglas
James R. Morgan

Kristin L. Johannsen

THOMSON

Australia · Canada · Mexico · Singapore · Spain · United Kingdom · United States

World Pass Advanced, Workbook
Susan Stempleski
James R. Morgan • *Nancy Douglas* • *Kristin L. Johannsen*

Publisher: Christopher Wenger
Director of Product Marketing: Amy Mabley
Director of Product Development: Anita Raducanu
Acquisitions Editor: Mary Sutton-Paul
Development Editor: Rebecca Klevberg
Sr. Print Buyer: Mary Beth Hennebury

International Marketing Manager: Ian Martin
Contributing Development Editor: Paul MacIntyre
Compositor: Parkwood Composition Service
Cover Designer: Christopher Hanzie, TYA Inc.
Printer: West Group

Printed in the United States.
1 2 3 4 5 6 7 8 9 10   09 08 07 06 05

For more information contact Thomson Heinle, 25 Thomson Place, Boston, MA 02210 USA, or you can visit our Internet site at **elt.thomson.com**

ISBN: 0-8384-2570-4

Photo Credits
4: IndexOpen/RF; **5:** © Hulton-Deutsch Collection/CORBIS; **8:** imagebroker/Alamy; **16:** Photos.com/RF; **18:** Photos.com/RF; **22:** Michael Setboun/Corbis; **28:** © Danita Delimont/Alamy; **34:** © Stapleton Collection/Corbis; **36:** top: © Jacky Naegelen/Reuters/Corbis; bottom: ©YVES HERMAN/Reuters/Corbis; **38:** © Matthias Kulka/CORBIS; **40:** © Brand X Pictures/Alamy; **46:** both: © TIM GRAHAM/Alamy; **52:** top: © Bob Krist/CORBIS; bottom: © Michael Nicholson/CORBIS; **59:** © Louie Psihoyos/CORBIS; **64:** © Michael Kim/Corbis; **70:** IndexOpen/RF

World Pass Advanced

Big Screen, Small Screen

Lesson A | Feature films

1 VOCABULARY & EXPRESSIONS

A Complete the sentences with words and expressions from the box, making all necessary changes.

> blockbuster   tearjerker   strike a compromise   wholesome
> B-movie   give away   mainstream

1. I love action movies, but my girlfriend only likes comedies so we always have to _____ when we want to see a film.

2. During the children's hour on TV, the networks broadcast only _____ educational programs that all ages can watch.

3. I love watching old _____ with plastic monsters and silly costumes. They're so funny!

4. A _____ movie is usually very expensive to make, but it is so popular that it makes all the money back and much more besides.

5. Tell me about the new Tom Cruise movie, but don't _____ the ending. I'm going to see it with my sister on Friday.

6. A _____ movie is a typical movie with famous actors and a somewhat predictable story.

7. I don't understand why people enjoy _____. Real life is full of enough problems—why see movies that make you cry?

B What do you think of these types of movies? Give your response in a complete sentence.

> **Example:** indie movies
> I haven't really seen many of them because they're not really popular in my country.

1. blockbusters

_____

2. romantic comedies

_____

3. wholesome family movies

_____

4. tearjerkers

_____

C When would you say it? Match the expression with the situation.

1. Why do you say that? _____   a. to request clarification
2. Can I just say something here? _____   b. to bring other people into a discussion
3. We only have five minutes left. _____   c. to bring a discussion to a conclusion
4. Let's see what someone else has to say. _____   d. to ask the reason for an opinion
5. To get back to our topic . . . _____   e. to interrupt in a discussion
6. Sorry, I'm not sure I understand. _____   f. to get people to return to the subject

2 GRAMMAR

A Complete the sentences with *so, such, so much,* or *so many.*

1. I have _____ homework tonight that I'm afraid I can't go to the movie with you. Sorry!

2. My hometown is _____ small that I know everyone there by name.

3. Jenny caught _____ a bad cold that she had to stay in bed for a week.

4. Yesterday, I got _____ e-mail messages that it took me all afternoon to answer them.

5. Andrea speaks English _____ well that many people think she's a native speaker.

6. Jorge has had _____ serious problems with his boss that he's thinking of quitting his job.

7. The dentist said the reason I have _____ terrible teeth is because I eat _____ sugar.

8. That mystery novel was _____ interesting that I stayed up until 4 A.M. reading it.

B Answer the questions using *such* or *so.*

Example: What kind of cook are you?
I'm such a bad cook that my friends won't come to my house for dinner.

1. How much money do some movie stars have?

_____

2. What kind of teacher did you have for your last English class?

_____

3. Is it easy to get a driver's license in your country?

_____

4. Do you have a little or a lot of free time?

_____

5. How old is the oldest person you've ever talked to?

_____

6. How many times have you seen your favorite movie?

_____

7. Did you have a good time on your last birthday?

_____

8. Was this exercise easy or difficult?

_____

C Write true sentences about yourself and your interests with these *-ed* and *-ing* adjectives.

1. fascinating _____.

2. disappointed _____.

3. entertaining _____.

4. shocked _____.

5. exciting _____.

Big Screen, Small Screen

| *Lesson B* | TV time |

1 READING

A Read the article about the history of television.

The History of Television

1   On January 27, 1926, a group of scientists, including members of Britain's Royal Institution, gathered in a laboratory in an upstairs room in London. **They** were about to witness the world's first television broadcast.

2   The television itself was little more than a collection of old junk taken from discarded machinery: a large cardboard disc with pieces of glass around it, behind which were several old electric motors and a mass of glass tubes and other parts from old radio receivers.

3   The engineer who had assembled this device was John Logie Baird, a slim, nervous man in his late thirties, who sat turning the knobs on a small control panel. Seated in the world's first TV studio—a chair in front of the cardboard disc—was a sixteen-year-old boy. You could say **he** was the world's first TV star.

4   As the boy turned his head from side to side, Baird focused and tuned his TV transmitter until the audience could see the image of the boy speaking and moving on a receiver in the same room. Then the audience moved to a separate room, and Baird repeated the demonstration with another receiver **there**—the first actual TV broadcast. To be truthful, the image on the receivers was faint and difficult to see, but Baird's "televisor" showed for the first time that it was possible to send and reproduce live images.

5   In June 1928, Baird transmitted the first outdoor television broadcast, and on August 22 of **the same year**, the General Electric Corporation in the United States produced the first televised news report. It showed the governor of New York accepting the Democratic Party's nomination for president.

6   A number of technical difficulties remained to be worked out, and it was not until 1936 that the first scheduled broadcasting service began. It was produced by the British Broadcasting Corporation in London. In **that same year**, the Radio Corporation of America, which later became RCA Corporation, installed experimental television receivers in 150 New York City homes and began its first transmissions. Their first program was a cartoon called *Felix the Cat*. Three years later, the National Broadcasting Corporation established regular TV broadcasts in the United States. The United States entered World War II in 1941, and broadcasting was suspended until after the war ended in 1945.

7   These first TVs looked very little like the ones we now have. The earliest TVs were large wooden cabinets with screens that measured only 7 to 10 inches (18 to 25 centimeters) diagonally. Today, 27-inch (69-centimeter) screens are very common, and conventional televisions are available with screens as large as 40 inches (100 centimeters). In the 1990s, rear-projection televisions became popular, with screens from 48 inches to 60 inches (122 centimeters to 155 centimeters) diagonally. There are also television sets with screens only 3 inches across—small enough to carry in your pocket.

8   Many of us today would find it difficult to imagine life without television, but the history of **this medium** is not a long one. Will its future development be equally rapid?

B Circle the correct answer.

1. What was John Logie Baird's big achievement?
   a. He produced the first TV show.
   b. He was the first actor on TV.
   c. He built the first working television.
   d. He produced the first news broadcast.

2. Which of these statements about the first television is NOT true?
   a. It was very expensive to build.
   b. Its picture was low in quality.
   c. It was made in England.
   d. It could show motion.

3. Who broadcast the first TV news report?
   a. the British Broadcasting Corporation
   b. John Logie Baird
   c. the General Electric Corporation
   d. the Democratic Party

4. In what year was the public first able to watch TV programs regularly?
   a. 1926
   b. 1928
   c. 1929
   d. 1936

5. What was "televisor" an early word for?
   a. a TV actor
   b. a TV set
   c. a TV announcer
   d. a TV program

6. Where did people watch the first TV broadcast?
   a. in their homes
   b. at the company's office
   c. outdoors
   d. in a laboratory

C Find this information in the reading.

1. the name of an early TV program _____

2. the location of the first TV broadcast _____

3. the largest size of TV screen mentioned _____

4. four things used to build the first TV set _____

   _____

D What do these words and phrases in bold refer to?

1. They (par. 1) _____

2. it (par. 2) _____

3. he (par. 3) _____

4. there (par. 4) _____

5. the same year (par. 5) _____

6. that same year (par. 6) _____

7. this medium (par. 8) _____

Essays: The thesis statement

Every good essay contains a thesis statement, usually in the first paragraph (introduction). The thesis statement is a sentence that expresses the main idea of your essay. It includes the topic as well as your opinion or attitude about the topic. Because it contains an opinion, readers could disagree with it. The essay tells readers why they should agree with this opinion.

A **Read these thesis statements. In each one, circle the essay's topic and underline the writer's opinion or attitude toward the topic.**

1. Watching television is not a waste of time.

2. Banning cars from the city center would solve many urban problems.

3. My city has some of the world's most interesting tourist attractions.

4. Poor diet is a major cause of many serious health problems.

5. Knowing a foreign language can be a big advantage when looking for a job.

B **Are these good thesis statements? Answer *Yes* or *No*.**

1. Many movies are produced in Hollywood. _____

2. Too many Hollywood movies today are boring and predictable. _____

3. Movies are a healthy form of escape from everyday stress. _____

4. Kids should be allowed to see any movies they want. _____

5. The three best movies I've seen. _____

6. Hollywood is not the best place for young filmmakers to start their careers. _____

7. I visited Hollywood on a trip to California last year. _____

8. The effects of violent movies on young children. _____

9. The government must do more to support filmmakers in our country. _____

10. I am going to describe my favorite movie. _____

C **You are going to write an essay about one of the best (or worst!) movies ever made. First, plan your essay.**

Title of movie: _____

Circle: Best / Worst

Thesis statement: _____

_____

Reason 1: _____

Details of Reason 1: _____

_____

_____

Reason 2: _____

Details of Reason 2: _____

_____

_____

D **Now write your essay in four paragraphs. Include the thesis statement in the introduction.**

Par. 1: Introduction—Introduce the movie and give your opinion.

Par. 2: Discuss the first reason for your opinion.

Par. 3: Discuss the second reason for your opinion.

Par. 4: Conclusion—Should readers see this movie?

1 VOCABULARY & EXPRESSIONS

A Complete the TV review by filling in each blank with one of the items from the box.

hypnotic	landscape	atmosphere	household names	relish
firsthand	take in	guaranteed	relatively	bustling

TV Tonight: *World Wanderers*

The first episode of *World Wanderers* takes us to Norway for a **(1)**_____ look at the country's beautiful west coast. It starts in the **(2)**_____ harbor town of Bergen, where we dine at the busy fish market before setting off on a cruise through Norway's world-famous fjords. This is a **(3)**_____ well-known destination, with hundreds of thousands of visitors every year, but it's still full of surprises. The unique **(4)**_____ of mountains that rise straight up from the sea is truly **(5)**_____. It's a lot to **(6)**_____. The only negative point about the show is it's just thirty minutes, too short to really **(7)**_____ everything we're seeing. But the producers do a good job of conveying the **(8)**_____ of each place we visit.

In the future, the show promises a mix of destinations—from **(9)**_____, like Paris and the Pyramids of Egypt, to new discoveries, like the Indonesian island of Lombok. It's **(10)**_____ to make you want to take a trip!

B Complete the sentences using your own ideas.

1. To me, _____ is <u>priceless</u> because _____
_____.

2. Sometimes I feel <u>powerless</u> about _____ because
_____.

3. Asking "_____?" is a <u>meaningless</u> question because
_____.

4. For me, _____ sometimes feels <u>effortless</u> because _____
_____.

C Read the phone conversation and complete the expressions.

Operator: Thank you for calling Golden Tours. How **(1)** _____ I **(2)**_____ your call?

Rafael: I'd like some information about your tours to Hawaii.

Operator: One **(3)**_____, please.

Agent: Good afternoon, **(4)**_____ is Wayne. **(5)**_____ may I **(6)** _____ you?

Rafael: Could you please (7)_____ me the (8)_____ of the tour to Hawaii that was in your newspaper ad?

Agent: Prices start at just $3,000.

Rafael: Oh . . . I'm (9)_____ that's a little (10)_____ of my price range.

Agent: In that case, you might be interested in one of our budget tours. We offer . . .

2 GRAMMAR

A Match each sentence with the function of the underlined past modal phrase.

1. You <u>must have</u> spent a lot of time in England because you have a British accent. _____

2. I <u>shouldn't have</u> eaten the whole cake. I feel sick! _____

3. I <u>could have</u> cooked something for dinner, but we decided to go out for pizza. _____

4. Jessica <u>might have</u> forgotten that we have a meeting now. _____

5. I <u>would have</u> helped you with your computer, but you didn't ask me. _____

6. Frank <u>couldn't have</u> written this report all by himself. It's 200 pages! _____

7. You <u>should have</u> called me on my cell phone instead of keeping me waiting. _____

a. making a strong suggestion in the past

b. expressing willingness in the past

c. making a conclusion about past events

d. expressing possibility in the past

e. talking about a possible explanation

f. expressing impossibility in the past

g. expressing regret about a past action that was taken

B Rewrite each sentence using a past modal phrase.

1. I was willing to give you a ride to the party, but I didn't know you were going.

_____.

2. It's possible that you left your dictionary on the train.

_____.

3. It was a very bad idea for Carla to speak to her boss that way.

_____.

4. I was probably taking a shower when you called because I didn't hear the phone.

_____.

5. It's not possible that Eric forgot about our date.

_____.

6. It was a good idea to review the vocabulary words before the test, but you didn't do it.

_____.

C Write true sentences about yourself using past modal phrases.

1. Write about a bad decision you made. (should have)

_____

2. Write about something you lost. What happened? (might have)

_____

3. Write about something that was possible in the past that you didn't try. (could have)

_____

4. Write about something you regret doing. (shouldn't have)

_____

The World Awaits You

| *Lesson B* | There and back |

1 READING

A Read this article about the founder of a travel guide company.

Travel Profile: Tony Wheeler, Publisher of *Lonely Planet* Travel Guides

1   When Tony Wheeler was ten years old, his parents asked him what he would like for a Christmas present. He asked for two things: a globe and a filing cabinet. Both were appropriate gifts for a boy who would grow up to head the world's largest travel publisher.

2   Today, Wheeler's company, *Lonely Planet* Publications, produces more than 650 different titles, covering destinations form Australia to Zimbabwe. Over six million copies annually are sold in 118 countries around the world. In other words, one in every four English-language guidebooks sold is a *Lonely Planet* guide.

3   In the early 1970s, Wheeler was a young engineer in England when he decided to take time off and see the world. He and his wife, Maureen, set off to travel through Asia to Australia, making the entire trip overland. When they reached Sydney, after nine months on the road, they found themselves **barraged** with the same questions over and over again: What kind of transportation did you use? What places did you take in? How much did it cost? Finally, Tony sat down at his kitchen table and wrote a ninety-four-page **pamphlet**, which he called "Across Asia on the Cheap." It gave details for the route they traveled from Europe across Turkey, Afghanistan, and India through to Australia. The Wheelers published it themselves, and were surprised and pleased when 8,500 copies were sold in bookstores across Australia.

4   From the sales of their book, the Wheelers earned enough money to spend another year traveling in Asia. At the end of 1974, they rented a room in an old **fleabag** hotel in Singapore and spent three months writing "South-East Asia on a Shoestring." The "yellow Bible" was an instant success; and after twelve editions, its cover is still yellow. When their India guidebook was published in 1980, it sold 100,000 copies, and the Wheelers found themselves heading a major business **enterprise**.

5   Surprisingly, Wheeler still spends a lot of time on the road, traveling and doing firsthand research for new guidebooks. Over 120 writers actually produce the books, but Wheeler himself relishes staying involved. Last year, he traveled to Shanghai, Singapore, Finland, the Baltic countries, Poland, Italy, Switzerland, Germany, Iceland, and Japan. He even found time to take a multicountry safari in Africa.

6   "I still do some writing every year," he says. "I've been involved in a couple of writing projects recently. More of the travel, though, is because I want to go to places, and there are things I want to see. We call it 'quality control,' just taking the books and trying them out."

7   Wheeler has been traveling since a **tender age**. His father was an airport manager for a British aviation company, and every few years the family was posted to a new country. They lived in Pakistan, the Bahamas, Canada, the United States, and England. Because he seldom spent two years at the same school, young Tony grew accustomed to being a foreigner.

8   After thirty years in the business, Wheeler admits that the *Lonely Planet* guidebooks have changed **drastically**. "When we started we were in our early twenties and writing books for people also in their early twenties, who were penniless. Now the business is so much bigger—there are so many more people traveling. Travel is now thought of more as something that's a right rather than a privilege."

9   Wheeler still strives to raise awareness of the effects that travel has on the world. "There's no question that tourism can be damaging on all sorts of levels. I think that people involved in the industry and those traveling have to be very aware of that and act accordingly. Although it is an activity that's sustainable, we have to think very carefully about how to make it work."

B Write the paragraph number next to the description.

1. Most recent trips _____
2. Wheeler's philosophy of tourism _____
3. How *Lonely Planet* became a success _____
4. The Wheelers' first publication _____
5. An international childhood _____
6. Why Wheeler still travels _____
7. Facts about *Lonely Planet* _____
8. A boy with big dreams _____
9. How the guidebooks are different now _____

C Locate this information in the reading.

1. Wheeler's original occupation _____
2. The number of *Lonely Planet* guidebooks sold every year _____
3. Two cities that Wheeler visited last year _____
4. The title of the Wheelers' first guide _____
5. The year they produced a guidebook to India _____
6. An Asian country where Wheeler lived as a child _____
7. The number of writers that *Lonely Planet* employs _____
8. The number of different books that *Lonely Planet* publishes _____

D Find the meaning of the boldfaced items in the reading from their context.

1. A **pamphlet** is ___.

   a. a short book   b. a kind of magazine   c. a map

2. A **fleabag** hotel is ___.

   a. very luxurious   b. cheap and uncomfortable   c. in the jungle

3. If someone is at a **tender age**, they are ___.

   a. young   b. middle-aged   c. elderly

4. A business **enterprise** is ___.

   a. an executive   b. a regulation   c. a company

5. If you are **barraged** with questions, people ask you ___.

   a. rudely   b. many times   c. gently

6. If something changes **drastically**, the change is ___.

   a. extreme   b. slow   c. unimportant

2 WRITING

A Read this article that was submitted to a student travel magazine. The mistakes have been underlined. Mark the type of mistake above each one, using the symbols in the box.

Sp	spelling	VT	verb tense
WF	word form	WW	wrong word
P	punctuation	WO	word order
X	word(s) missing	??	I don't understand this.

Too many visitors to South Korea spend all of their time in Seoul. In order to really understand my country's culture and four thousand **(1)** <u>year</u> of history, you **(2)** <u>had better</u> visit the city of Gyeongju.

Gyeongju **(3)** _____ which is located in the southern part of the country, was the **(4)** <u>cappitol</u> of the ancient kingdom of Silla for almost a thousand years. It was the center of the arts, science, and government in a very **(5)** <u>wealth</u> country. In the Gyeongju National Museum you **(6)** <u>would</u> see the gold crowns of the Silla kings and queens and learn about the people's comfortable way of life.

In many ways, Gyeongju is **(7)** <u>likes</u> an open-air museum. All around the city, there are ancient palaces and temples. The kings and queens of Silla are **(8)** <u>bury</u> in huge tombs that look like hills covered with green grass. Just outside of the city is a mountain called Namsan. The forest there is filled with ancient statues and temples, and you can spend days just hiking in it. Tourists can also rent bicycles to ride through the countryside and visit more **(9)** <u>sites ancient</u>. One of **(10)** _____ most beautiful is Seokguram, a statue of the Buddha built inside a stone cave.

Visitors who come to Gyeongju will see a different side of Korea. Today, it's a modern country, but you will soon see why Gyeongju was called the "City of Gold" long ago.

B Correct each of the mistakes in the article.

1. _____   6. _____
2. _____   7. _____
3. _____   8. _____
4. _____   9. _____
5. _____   10. _____

C Now write your own travel article about a destination that visitors to your country will enjoy. Include an introduction to attract your readers' interest, one or two body paragraphs of information about the destination, and a conclusion that pulls the article together.

1 VOCABULARY & EXPRESSIONS

A Match these words and phrases with their meanings.

1. sleep deprivation _____
2. stick to _____
3. hectic _____
4. cope with _____
5. bond with _____
6. mishap _____
7. rash _____
8. compulsory _____
9. apprehensive _____
10. sign up for _____
11. expectation _____

a. hurried, excessively busy
b. follow a plan or a promise
c. register yourself, enroll
d. deal successfully with a difficult situation
e. what you believe or hope will happen
f. nervous or fearful
g. sudden, without proper planning
h. form a close relationship with someone
i. required for everyone
j. minor accident without serious results
k. feeling extremely tired from lack of rest

B Complete the sentences with the correct form of a word from the box. Use each word only once.

accept	except	pass	past	lose
advise	advice	affect	effect	loose

1. I went on a diet and lost fifteen pounds, and now I have to buy a lot of new clothes. My favorite jeans are too _____ to wear!

2. Jameela applied to four different universities, and she was _____ at all of them. Now she faces a tough decision.

3. The topic of my essay is the negative _____ of smoking on health.

4. My professor _____ me to take a special course this summer.

5. Jason _____ his driving test the first time he took it, and now he's driving his parents' car everywhere.

6. Min-Chul spent the _____ year studying for his university entrance exam.

7. I'm really enjoying all of my classes, _____ biology. I'm not very interested in science.

8. I think you really should quit your part-time job. Working at night is starting to _____ your grades.

9. I can never remember where I put my cell phone. I _____ it at least once a day!

10. This book contains a lot of good _____ on how to improve your English fluency.

C Imagine you're at an interview. Write one phrase could you use in each situation.

1. The interviewer asks a question, and you need to think about your answer.

   _____.

2. You're not sure what the interviewer meant in a question.

   _____.

3. You're not satisfied with your answer, and you want to say it differently.

   _____.

2 GRAMMAR

A Fill in the correct form of the verb. Some are negative.

1. Your new cell phone has really small keys. Do you wish you _____ (buy) it?

2. On exam day, a lot of students wish they _____ (study) harder.

3. My brother lives overseas. I really wish you _____ (meet) him.

4. Eva wishes she _____ (find) a better job soon because her salary is very low.

5. I got angry at my boyfriend last night, and now I really wish I _____ (say) such mean things to him.

6. Luis wishes the other students in the dorm _____ (be) quieter. They listen to loud music almost every night.

7. It's raining harder now. I wish I _____ (bring) my umbrella.

8. Alex was absent yesterday. The teacher wishes he _____ (miss) class.

9. I wish I _____ (be) so sleepy in the morning. I often miss the bus and get to class late.

10. Yong-min has to work late tonight. I wish he _____ (go) to the movie with us.

B Write sentences about your own wishes and hopes for these things.

1. your English class _____.

   _____.

2. your city _____.

   _____.

3. the environment _____.

   _____.

4. future technology _____.

   _____.

C Fill in the spaces with the correct form of a verb from the box.

> hope   wish   make   allow   let

1. When I was a child, my parents always _____ me finish my homework before watching TV.

2. I really _____ we'll have good weather for our trip to the beach this weekend.

3. I think teachers should _____ us to use our dictionaries when we take an exam.

4. My neighbor plays the piano really badly. I _____ he would take some lessons!

5. My boss _____ me take a day off on Monday because I worked on the weekend.

6. In my opinion, you shouldn't _____ children eat foods they don't like.

7. Carla bought a desktop computer, but now she really _____ she had gotten a laptop.

8. No dogs are _____ in any of the city parks.

School and Beyond

| *Lesson B* | New school, old school |

1 READING

A Read this article about crossover teachers.

From **Cubicle** to Classroom

June Diaz had it all. She enjoyed her work as a public relations specialist at Arrow Communications, a firm in Miami. She had been with her company for almost ten years, and she had received several promotions during that time. Her clients loved the magazines and reports she produced for them. But, somehow, she just couldn't get an old dream out of her head.

"I always wanted to be a teacher," she says. "When I was a little kid, I used to play school with all my friends. I stood in front and made them recite their lessons." In high school, she started a volunteer tutoring service to help elementary school kids in low-income neighborhoods with their homework. But, when she started college, her parents talked her out of majoring in education, saying there was "no money in it." Instead, she earned a business degree. "I wish I hadn't listened," she says today.

Today, Diaz is following her dream. She enrolled last year in a special program at Atlantic Coastal University that allows professionals to become teachers in only a year by taking special courses. She is one of a growing number of "crossover teachers" in the United States—people who have left their former careers to go into the classroom. Among them are nurses who became science teachers and office managers who teach math. According to the National Center for Education Information in Washington, over 200,000 new teachers were trained in this type of program in the first six years the courses were offered.

In the past, regulations about who could teach in America's public schools were much more **rigid.** Only graduates with a four-year degree in education could qualify, and candidates had to go through a lengthy **bureaucratic** process of certification. But in the 1980s, many cities were experiencing a **drastic** shortage of teachers, and they began looking for new ways to **recruit** people who truly wanted to teach. Programs to train crossover teachers have helped ease the shortage.

Daniel Feldstein was the supervisor of public schools in New York City, one of the first cities to hire crossover teachers. "These are people who believe teaching is a calling," he says. "It's not just a job. They're incredibly dedicated." He says that students really enjoy having teachers with a broad experience of the world— someone who has had another career before coming to the classroom.

Not everyone supports the idea, however. "These crossover teachers have far less training than their colleagues do," points out Lauretta Coggs, president of the National Association of Teachers. "And when they are forty years old, they may have only one or two years of teaching experience compared with a professional teacher who has already been in the classroom for almost twenty years. There's no substitute for experience."

Some parents also express doubts about this new **breed** of teachers. "My son's social studies teacher used to be a banker," says Natalia Chen. "I'm sure he knows a lot about money, but does he really know how kids learn best?"

It's not easy becoming a crossover teacher. Most continue to work at their **previous** jobs while taking courses, resulting in hectic schedules. After completing part of their course work, they also do practice teaching, working in an actual classroom supervised by an experienced teacher. This requires **candidates** to arrange for one day off from work at their regular job every week.

Diaz recently had her first day of practice teaching, working with second graders at a nearby elementary school. "I'm teaching reading and math. I'm having the time of my life, and I haven't even graduated yet!"

B Read the statements and circle *T* for *true*, *F* for *false*, or *NI* for *no information*. Change the false sentences to make them true.

1. Crossover teachers must study for four years to become qualified.   T F NI

2. In high school, June Diaz started a tutoring service.   T F NI

3. June Diaz earned a bachelor's degree in education.   T F NI

4. June Diaz was unhappy with her job at Arrow Communications.   T F NI

5. People from different fields have become crossover teachers.   T F NI

6. Many American states have a problem with too many qualified teachers.   T F NI

7. The number of crossover teachers is falling.   T F NI

8. Most parents accept the idea of crossover teachers.   T F NI

9. June Diaz has already started teaching.   T F NI

10. New York was one of the first cities to hire crossover teachers.   T F NI

11. Teachers in the United States all have the same kind of training.   T F NI

12. June Diaz plans to get a job in an elementary school.   T F NI

C Answer in your own words.

1. What are crossover teachers? _____.

_____.

2. How do people become crossover teachers? _____.

_____.

3. Why do people become crossover teachers? _____.

_____.

4. Who supports this program? Why? _____.

5. Who disagrees with this program? Why? _____.

_____.

D Find the boldfaced words in the reading with these meanings. (Hint: There is one in the title).

1. involving complicated official rules _____

2. earlier _____

3. type or kind _____

4. people who are trying for a position _____

5. a small section of an office, for one person _____

6. strict and unchanging _____

7. severe, serious _____

8. find and hire people for a job _____

A You are going to write an opinion essay about the advantages and disadvantages of crossover teachers. Reread the article on page 16.

B List these ideas in the correct column. Add as many others as you can to each column—both ideas from the reading and your own ideas.

have less training
are very enthusiastic
can be hired quickly

Advantages of Crossover Teachers

Disadvantages of Crossover Teachers

C Plan and write your opinion essay about crossover teachers, using information from the article and ideas you listed in the chart above.

Par. 1: Introduction—What are crossover teachers?

Par. 2: Advantages of crossover teachers

Par. 3: Disadvantages of crossover teachers

Par. 4: Conclusion—Are crossover teachers a good idea for your country? Why, or why not?

Contemporary Issues

Lesson A | In the city

1 VOCABULARY & EXPRESSIONS

A Read the article on illegal brand-name copying and fill in the spaces with the correct form of a word or expression from the box.

> mediocre   panic   monopoly   greedy   compensate
> crack down   take to court   pending   consumer   churn out
> rip off   unauthorized   emerging

Last week, the government announced that it was **(1)** _____ on manufacturers who produce **(2)** _____ copies of brand-name fashions such as shoes, bags, and watches. The announcement caused **(3)** _____ among many small shopkeepers in Central Market. One manufacturer of fake luxury brand name watches has already been **(4)** _____, and several other cases are **(5)** _____, with decisions expected soon.

The makers of genuine fashion products believe that they should be **(6)** _____ for the money they have lost to illegal manufacturers. "These illegal manufacturers must not be allowed to **(7)** _____ millions of copies of the designs that we work so hard to produce," says James Torres, president of the Fashion Industry Council. "It's especially a problem for **(8)** _____ designers who are just starting out in the field. Furthermore, the quality of these products is **(9)** _____, and it gives the public a bad impression."

(10) _____ who shop for brand-name fashions have different opinions. Some support the government's campaign. "Dishonest stores can **(11)** _____ customers by selling them fake merchandise," says Lori Miller. But Josh Richards disagrees with the campaign. "The real problem is that these fashion companies are too **(12)** _____ for money and fame. They have a **(13)** _____ on their business so they can charge any crazy price they want."

B Match the parts of these expressions for giving your opinion.

1. Without _____   a. that, but

2. Take _____   b. besides

3. Not to mention _____   c. an idea

4. I'm _____   d. the fact that

5. To give you _____   e. a doubt

6. Not only _____   f. for example

7. And _____   g. convinced that

A Complete each sentence with a clause from the box.

1. If I weren't so tired, _____.

2. If I hadn't had an exam the next day, _____.

3. If I ate breakfast, _____.

4. If I hadn't studied so much, _____.

5. If I had left earlier, _____.

6. If I had gone to the store last night, _____.

7. If I had a day off, _____.

I wouldn't be so hungry in class   I would sleep until noon   I wouldn't need to go today I would go to Leslie's party tonight   I wouldn't have gotten such a good grade I would have gone to the movie with you   I wouldn't have missed my bus

B Which sentences in Activity A are about the present? _____

Which sentences in Activity A are about the past? _____

C Fill in the correct form of each verb. All are unreal situations in the past.

1. If I (know) _____ you were sick last week, I (visit) _____ you.

2. We (go) _____ with you to the theme park on Saturday if we (have) _____ enough money.

3. If Beth (not study) _____ all night, she (not pass) _____ her computer programming test.

4. You (meet) _____ my new boyfriend if you (come) _____ to the party last weekend.

5. If you (listen) _____ to your friends' advice, you (not have) _____ so many problems.

6. Marianne (go) _____ to National University if she (get) _____ a better score on the entrance exam.

7. I (send) _____ you a postcard from Australia if you (give) _____ me your address!

D Write your own sentences about the results of these unreal situations.

1. (you started learning English at two years of age)

_____.

_____.

2. (you were the oldest/youngest/only child in your family)

_____.

_____.

School and Beyond

| *Lesson B* | Conflict resolution |

1 READING

A Read this article about the problem of homeless children.

Children of the Streets

Homeless people are a tragic sight in the cities of nearly every country in the world, but the ones in the most difficult situation are the street children. Today, at least fifty million children struggle to survive without a home or parents to support them. No one knows the exact number of homeless children, because they often fear and avoid authorities. Some have run away from home because of family problems, while others have been forced to leave home because their parents simply lacked enough money to support them. They manage to survive through hard work, luck, and courage. Here are the stories of three street children.

Dolgion is fourteen years old. He lives in Ulaanbaatar, the capital of the central Asian country Mongolia. When he was seven, his family's home burned down, and they were forced to move in with relatives. His mother left to find work in another city, and then one day his father disappeared. Finally, Dolgion was asked to leave because his relatives couldn't afford to feed him. Since then, he has made his home with a group of other street children in an underground hole for heating pipes. During the day, they collect empty bottles to sell, and together they earn about two dollars a day. If there's any leftover money after they buy noodles for their evening meal, they spend it playing computer games in a PC game room. His dreams? "When I grow up," he says, "I will own a bottle-collection point. And I will find my parents. I will buy a house, and we will all live together."

Rukshana and her little sister sleep under a bridge in Mumbai, India. Rukshana, who is fifteen, tries to earn enough money to support both of them so that eleven-year-old Deepa will be able to go to school. Every morning during rush hour, she boards the commuter trains from the suburbs to the central city and spends the entire day selling hair ornaments and magazines to women traveling to work. If the police catch her, she will have to pay a fine—more money than she earns in a week. The girls' parents both died several years ago, and their older brother lives in a faraway village and has five children of his own that he struggles to support. But, their life is not all hardship. At least three times a week, the two sisters go to see a movie—they especially love family dramas. In the future, Rukshana wants learn to read and write. "Then I will get a proper house—make something of my life and show people. I will have some gold jewelry of my own. Then my life will be stable."

Jack, who is only twelve, and looks even younger, is a tiny, thin boy with tired eyes. He earns his living by cleaning passengers' shoes on public transportation in the streets of Manila. It's exhausting work, and he earns only three dollars a day. "I don't know how many shoes I have to wipe to earn it," he says. "I get kicked on my back by some of the passengers." On days he is unable to earn enough money this way, he is forced to beg in the park where he sleeps. Jack was forced to leave the home he shared with his mother, brothers, and sisters in order to earn a living. He misses them terribly and hopes to be reunited with them. He likes to draw pictures when he can't express his feelings in words: "This house is for me and my brothers and sisters," he says. "Some of them would study, and some would guard the house. That's the kind of life I want to have."

B Complete the chart with information from the reading. Write short notes, not complete sentences.

	Dolgion	Rukshana	Jack
Age			
Country			
Family Background			
Reason for Homelessness			
How They Support Themselves			
Future Hopes			

C Answer the questions.

1. What obstacles do these children face? _____
_____
_____.

2. Do you think any of these children will achieve their dreams? _____ Why, or why not? _____
_____
_____.

3. What surprised you in this article? _____
_____
_____.

When writing about your opinion, you should support your argument with details and facts, in order to persuade your readers to agree with your opinion.

A Read each opinion. Mark the statement that does NOT support the opinion.

1. University students should be allowed to choose all of their courses, without requirements.

   _____ a. Students are all individuals with their own needs and interests.

   _____ b. One program can't meet the needs of every student.

   _____ c. A modern university offers a tremendous variety of courses.

2. Nuclear power plants are not a good energy option for the future.

   _____ a. Many countries have stopped building new nuclear power plants.

   _____ b. Their cost is very high in comparison with other ways to produce electricity.

   _____ c. There is a possibility of devastating accidents if they malfunction.

3. Free music downloads from the Internet bring more benefits than problems.

   _____ a. They give emerging musicians a chance to reach new audiences.

   _____ b. Consumers often find new music that they enjoy and will later buy it.

   _____ c. This practice is unfair to artists, who have to work hard to earn a living.

4. Parents need to control the amount of time that their children spend online.

   _____ a. Kids who don't get enough outdoor play easily become overweight.

   _____ b. Children become socially isolated if they spend all their time with online friends.

   _____ c. The cost of a new computer is far too high for many families in this country.

5. The manufacture and sale of cigarettes should be banned in this country.

   _____ a. Last year, over 50,000 citizens died from diseases caused by smoking.

   _____ b. Two of the largest companies in the country are cigarette producers.

   _____ c. Precious farmland is wasted on production of a crop that actually harms people.

B Complete each of these statements by circling your opinion. Then give three reasons to support this opinion.

1. Students in our country (should/should not) be required to learn a foreign language in high school.

   a. _____

   b. _____

   c. _____

2. There (should/should not) be a law requiring people to wear their seat belts in cars.

   a. _____

   b. _____

   c. _____

3. Our country (should/should not) encourage more foreign tourists to come here.

   a. _____

   b. _____

   c. _____

C Write short replies to these two messages, agreeing or disagreeing with them. Be sure to support your opinion with reasons.

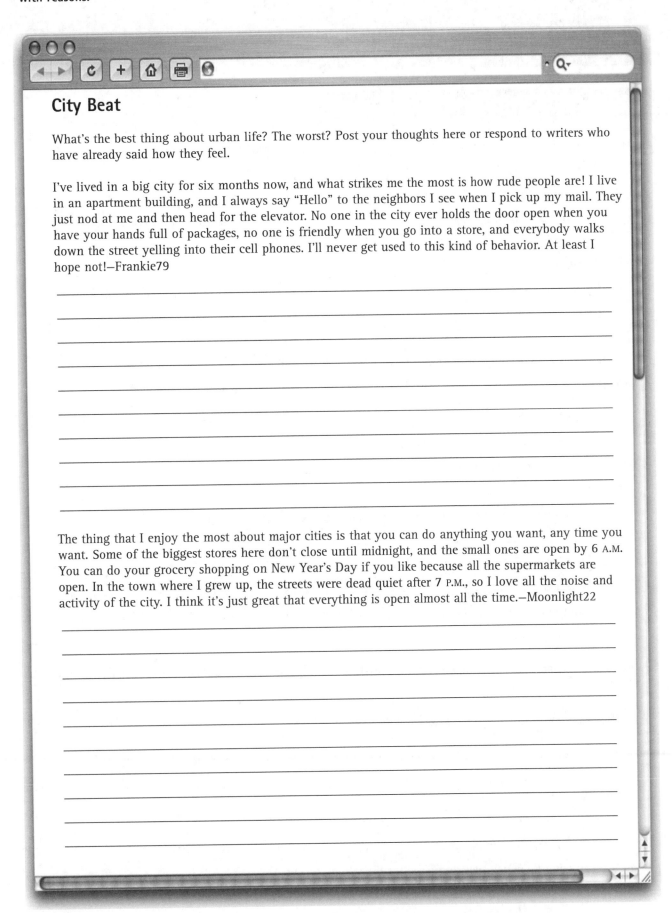

City Beat

What's the best thing about urban life? The worst? Post your thoughts here or respond to writers who have already said how they feel.

I've lived in a big city for six months now, and what strikes me the most is how rude people are! I live in an apartment building, and I always say "Hello" to the neighbors I see when I pick up my mail. They just nod at me and then head for the elevator. No one in the city ever holds the door open when you have your hands full of packages, no one is friendly when you go into a store, and everybody walks down the street yelling into their cell phones. I'll never get used to this kind of behavior. At least I hope not!—Frankie79

The thing that I enjoy the most about major cities is that you can do anything you want, any time you want. Some of the biggest stores here don't close until midnight, and the small ones are open by 6 A.M. You can do your grocery shopping on New Year's Day if you like because all the supermarkets are open. In the town where I grew up, the streets were dead quiet after 7 P.M., so I love all the noise and activity of the city. I think it's just great that everything is open almost all the time.—Moonlight22

In Other Words

1 VOCABULARY & EXPRESSIONS

A Form sentences by matching the columns to show the meaning of the underlined words.

1. If you <u>convey</u> an idea, _____
2. If you are <u>proficient</u> in a language, _____
3. If you speak in <u>halting</u> way, _____
4. If you are <u>immersed</u> in a language, _____
5. If Arabic is your <u>primary language</u>, _____
6. If your English is <u>passable</u>, _____
7. If you <u>brush up on</u> your French, _____
8. If you <u>carry on</u> a conversation, _____
9. If Spanish is your <u>mother tongue</u>, _____
10. If you <u>master</u> Russian, _____
11. If you <u>retain</u> new words, _____

a. you don't forget them.
b. you listen to and respond to another person.
c. you learned it when you were a baby.
d. you speak it very well.
e. you communicate it to another person.
f. you practice it after not using it for a long time.
g. you speak it the best of all your languages.
h. you speak slowly with many mistakes.
i. you are in contact with it all day.
j. you learn to speak it very well.
k. you speak it fairly well.

B Answer the questions with your own ideas.

1. What do you do to <u>retain</u> new vocabulary words? _____
   _____

2. What are some situations where people are <u>immersed</u> in a foreign language? _____
   _____

3. How long would it take a foreign student to become <u>proficient</u> in your language? _____
   _____

4. What are some good ways to <u>brush up on</u> a language you studied a long time ago? _____
   _____

C Review the meanings of these acronyms and initialisms on page 53 of your Student Book. Then use them to complete the sentences.

> PIN   ASAP   AC   ATM   TBA   TGIF

1. We're having a _____ party after work at Sal's Pizza. Want to join us?

2. You shouldn't write your _____ number down because someone could find it and use it to access your bank account.

3. Could you turn the _____ on? It's really hot in here.

4. This form is very important. You need to fill it in and submit it _____.

5. We still don't know the time and place for the job interviews. They are _____.

6. I'll stop by the _____ on the way home from work and get some cash.

A Reduce the adverb clauses in these sentences.

1. Because she was interested in Chinese culture, Nina decided to study Mandarin.
   Being interested in Chinese culture, Nina decided to study Mandarin.

2. Since she had never studied a foreign language before, she didn't realize it was supposed to be difficult.
   _____.

3. She went to her Mandarin class every night after she finished work.
   _____.

4. Because she learned five new words every day, she soon developed a large vocabulary.
   _____.

5. After she had studied for two years, she took a trip to Beijing.
   _____.

6. Because she was able to carry on a conversation, she really enjoyed her time in China.
   _____.

B Combine the pairs of sentences with a reduced adverbial clause, using the word in parenthesis.

1. He took classes at night. He worked in a factory during the day. (while)
   While taking classes at night, he worked in a factory during the day.

2. We started this course. We've learned a lot of new vocabulary. (since)
   _____.

3. She graduated from college. She went to work for an airline. (after)
   _____.

4. I take a bath and brush my teeth. I go to bed. (before)
   _____.

C Are these sentences with reduced adverb clauses correct? Mark each one *C* for *correct* or *I* for *incorrect*. Rewrite the incorrect ones to make them logical.

Example: While walking on the beach, the waves were very big after the storm. _I_
While walking on the beach, I saw big waves after the storm.

1. Having been burned in a fire, the doctors treated the victim in the hospital. _____
   _____.

2. After leaving the office, Carla went to the post office to buy some stamps. _____
   _____.

3. Not wearing a coat, I felt very cold all day. _____
   _____.

4. Using a microscope, the deadly bacteria were easy to see. _____
   _____.

5. Riding my bicycle, a car swerved in front of me. _____
   _____.

6. Barking happily, Kevin played with his dog. _____
   _____.

In Other Words

1 READING

A Read this article about a language-learning experience

Studying Spanish in Guatemala
by Johanna Kristiansen

Can animals think? I had to **consider** this a moment before answering. "Si, creo que . . ."

Not your typical Spanish class topic, but this was not your typical Spanish class. My teacher and I sat at a table on a rooftop terrace, looking out over the city of Quetzaltenango, Guatemala. At the next table, another teacher and student were talking about recipes. This was only my second week of study.

I had come to Guatemala at the beginning of a trip through Central America, hoping to brush up on my college Spanish. I had plenty of company. Guatemala's dozens of Spanish language schools, some of the best and most inexpensive anywhere, draw students from around the world.

Though there are schools throughout the country, most are in two cities–Antigua and Quetzaltenango. Deciding to split my time between the two, I went first to Antigua, the old capital, which is a handsome city of colonial streets lined with brown and yellow houses. The city is surrounded by tall blue volcanoes, which erupt every few centuries.

It's not surprising that over 12,000 foreigners every year come to study in Antigua's language schools. Enrollment is simple and **straightforward**. One Saturday afternoon, I strolled into the office of a school that had been recommended to me, and on Monday morning, I began classes.

My teacher, Juan Cecilio, was incredibly patient with my halting Spanish. Seeing that I had forgotten the basics, he gave me a fast review of Spanish grammar in only five days. By the end of the week, we were talking (slowly) about Guatemalan history and the cost of living.

All of Antigua's schools follow a similar system. Students have four hours of **one-on-one** instruction with a teacher every morning. Afternoons are for extra lessons, sightseeing, or hanging out in the town's cafés. Classes run from Monday to Friday, and students have the **option** to change teachers each week.

Like most students, I chose homestay accommodation. My hosts, Luis and Angelina, had both lived in the United States, but our conversations were entirely in Spanish. Dinners with them were a great way to practice the language, and I learned about aspects of Guatemalan life that are invisible to the average tourist.

Quetzaltenango was a complete contrast. Usually called by its local name, Xela (shay-la), it is a busy commercial center, not a living museum. Many Spanish schools there sponsor community projects, such as schools and clinics, in the surrounding countryside. Casa Xelaju, where I studied, has tutoring programs for children in a nearby village, and many students volunteer.

Xela has three universities, and many of the city's Spanish teachers hold teaching degrees from one of them. Flori, the teacher I talked with on the rooftop, was a graduate in Spanish and history. By this time, I could **handle** some fairly complex topics, and our talks ranged from astrology to names of vegetables.

The best part of one-on-one teaching is that the daily lesson can be about anything you want. One day, another student and I asked our teachers to come with us to the Mayan market in a small village nearby. Together, the four of us asked questions and learned about the uses of the **medicinal** plants on sale and the **significance** of the traditional weaving designs.

Though most students stay for several months, every Friday afternoon is "graduation day" for those who are leaving, with a party and a cake. On the day I left Xela, several long-term students gave **tearful** goodbye speeches, telling moving stories of their volunteer work with village kids and good times with their host families. For now, I could only thank my teachers for helping me to put my thoughts into Spanish words—but in the back of my mind, I was already planning how to come back and really master the language.

B Find this information in the reading.

1. Which cities did the author study in? _____

2. Where had she studied Spanish before? _____

3. Why did she want to improve her Spanish? _____

_____.

4. How many students are in each class? _____

5. How many hours per week do students have class? _____

6. Where do students stay? _____

7. Who chooses the topics of the lessons? _____

8. What other activities can students do? _____

_____.

C Match the boldfaced words from the story with their meanings.

1. consider _____
2. medicinal _____
3. tearful _____
4. significance _____
5. handle _____
6. one-on-one _____
7. option _____
8. straightforward _____

a. without problems

b. cope with

c. choice, possibility

d. sad

e. think carefully about

f. individual

g. useful for treating disease

h. meaning, importance

D Give your opinion.

1. What are some good points of learning a language this way? _____

_____.

2. What are some bad points? _____

_____.

3. Would you like to take a language course like this? Why, or why not? _____

_____.

A Study these charts and write a paragraph explaining the information in each one. Review the expressions on page 56 in your Student Book.

1.

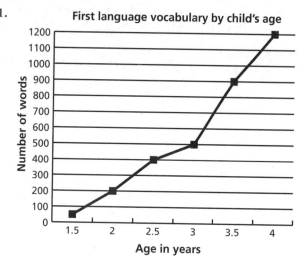

2.

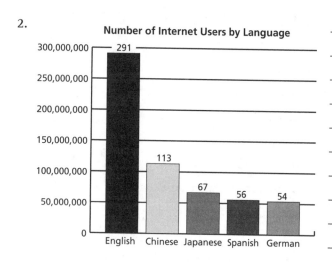

3.

Primary languages in Malaysia

English 5%

Indian 10%

Chinese 25%   Malay 60%

_____
_____
_____
_____
_____
_____
_____
_____
_____
_____
_____
_____
_____
_____

B Write a report about opportunities for students in your country to practice their English. Divide your report into sections and give each one a heading. Your report should answer these questions.

1. Overall, do students have enough opportunities to practice their English?

2. What opportunities do students have to practice listening and speaking?

3. What opportunities do students have to practice reading and writing?

4. What recommendations do you have for providing more opportunities for students?

1 VOCABULARY & EXPRESSIONS

A Complete the sentences with the correct form of a word or expression from the box.

sidetracked	storied	juggling	channel	have something in mind
cause a stir	aspirations	twinkle	bump into	renowned
swap	fixture	apprentice		

1. Single parents have to be experts at _____ their work and family responsibilities.

2. Dale worked as an _____ to a carpenter before he started his own construction business.

3. Dr. Clark is one the most _____ historians in our country.

4. When I was young, I had _____ of being an astronaut when I grew up.

5. Kayla really _____ in the office when she announced she was quitting.

6. Sorry I didn't call you on Friday like I promised. I meant to, but I got _____ with a lot of important e-mails.

7. When I was at the airport, I _____ an old classmate of mine who I hadn't seen in ten years.

8. These days, I'm _____ all my energy into starting a new career as a dance teacher.

9. I love to sit outside at night and watch the stars _____ in the sky.

10. Professor Mahmoud has been a _____ at the university for more than forty years.

11. I haven't decided what I'm going to do on my vacation yet, but I _____.

12. Laura Lane had a _____ career in the movies, and acted with all the greatest stars of the 1950s.

13. I often _____ clothes with my sister, because it's fun to wear something different for a change.

B Write replies using expressions with *hat*.

1. A: Is Ana shy about singing in front of people?

   B: No, not at all. She'll do it _____.

2. A: I'm getting a new job next month, but don't tell anyone.

   B: Don't worry. I'll _____.

3. A: I got 100% on the English exam!

   B: I have to _____ to you. It was really hard!

4. A: Jason is the owner of the restaurant, and also the chef.

   B: If he _____ like that, it must keep him really busy.

5. A: Did you hear that Jennifer Lopez has a new boyfriend?

   B: That rumor is totally _____. Tell me something I don't know!

A You had a long phone conversation with your aunt yesterday. Report the things she said, using the verbs in parentheses.

1. "What are you doing these days?" (ask)
   She asked me what I was doing these days.

2. "I've been spending a lot of time watching movies on TV." (say)
   _____.

3. "Your cousin Margaret is getting married next month." (tell)
   _____.

4. "When are you going to get married?" (ask)
   _____.

5. "My dog is getting fat." (mention)
   _____.

6. "You really shouldn't work so hard." (advise)
   _____.

7. "Please come over and have dinner with us on Sunday." (ask)
   _____.

8. "David and Lucy will be coming for dinner, too." (say)
   _____.

9. "Do you like baked ham?" (ask)
   _____.

10. "Remember to send your uncle a birthday card." (remind)
   _____.

B Match the reported sentence and the reason there is no tense change.

1. Joanne said she works at night _____
2. They said I should have gone to the movie. _____
3. My grandmother always said that silence is golden. _____
4. He said a minute ago that he isn't hungry. _____

a. something just said
b. habitual actions
c. accepted fact
d. should have/could have/past perfect

C Report each sentence. If no tense change is needed, tell the reason by writing *a, b, c,* or *d* from Activity B.

1. Alan: "I'm going to the coffee shop after class."
   _____.

2. Emily: "I run marathons every summer."
   _____.

3. Linda: "In 2002, I hadn't graduated yet."
   _____.

4. Harun: "People in India speak many languages."
   _____.

Ordinary People, Extraordinary Lives

| **Lesson B** | The kindness of strangers |

1 READING

A Read this story of a remarkable man.

Remarkable Lives: Lafcadio Hearn

The story sounds familiar. A young man, failing in his career, decides to make a fresh start overseas. He travels to Japan and gets a job teaching English at a college. There, he falls in love and gets married. He settles down with his Japanese wife, raises a family, and launches a successful new career writing about Japan.

What's surprising is that it all happened over one hundred years ago. The young man was an Irish writer named Lafcadio Hearn, who arrived in the Japanese city of Matsue in 1890. Over the next fourteen years, he wrote a dozen books about Japan and never left his adopted country. He even became a Japanese citizen, taking the name Yakumo Koizumi.

Born in 1850 and raised in Dublin, Hearn had led a difficult life before his journey to Japan. He was the son of an Irish military officer and a Greek woman, who went back to her country, **abandoning** her husband and child. When the army sent his father to India, Lafcadio went to live with an elderly aunt. At the age of sixteen, an accident left him blind in one eye. Soon after that, his aunt lost all her money in a bad investment and was forced to send Lafcadio to live with distant relatives in Cincinnati.

Hearn held a series of **menial** jobs, finally landing a position as a newspaper crime reporter at the *Cincinnati Enquirer*. Always a difficult character, Hearn frequently clashed with his editors and was forced to move on to newspapers in Memphis, New Orleans, and New York.

Then, in 1889, *Harper's Magazine* hired him to write a series of articles on Japan. Hearn arrived in Yokohama with two suitcases. In his essay "My First Day in the Orient," he wrote about the unfamiliar sights and sounds that greeted him, from the boom of a massive temple bell down to the tiny multicolored wrapper on a package of toothpicks.

Only days after arriving in Japan, Hearn got into a **dispute** with his publishers and lost his job. With the help of other foreigners, he managed to get a government appointment to teach English at a college in Matsue, a small city on Japan's west coast. He used the last of his money to get there.

He fell in love with Matsue and soon married a local woman. After years of wandering, he felt he had come home. He wrote with affection of the details of life in Matsui, like the stone fox statues in the Shinto shrine that he passed every morning on his way to school and the lovely sunsets over Lake Shinji in the center of the city.

As the only foreigner in remote Matsue, Hearn **immersed** himself in the Japanese way of life. He wore Japanese clothing, ate Japanese food, and lived in an old-fashioned Japanese house. With help from his wife, he collected and translated hundreds of traditional ghost stories. He traveled to tiny villages and ancient temples, recording everything he saw.

Many of the author's belongings are now preserved in his former home in Matsue. Alongside his books and pens are more personal treasures—his collection of Japanese tobacco pipes, a bamboo cage for his pet crickets, a seashell that his wife bought for him on an excursion. Visitors can see a stack of old newspapers with English lessons for his children written on them with a Japanese brush: "He is, she is, we are, you are good."

Hearn was writing at a **pivotal** time in Japanese history. The country was opening its doors to the modern world, and ways of life thousands of years old were changing fast. Electricity was replacing candlelight, and the first railroad line was crossing the country. In his books, he struggled to record traditional Japan before it disappeared.

Though Hearn's work has largely been forgotten, we owe a great deal to the remarkable man who first introduced the rich culture of traditional Japan to the world.

B Circle *T* for *true* or *F* for *false*. Write the phrase or sentence from the reading that supports your answer.

1. Hearn was a very successful writer in the United States.   T   F

_____.

2. Hearn often had trouble getting along with people.   T   F

_____.

3. Hearn had serious problems with his vision.   T   F

_____.

4. Hearn adjusted easily to life in his new country.   T   F

_____.

5. Hearn's books are very popular today.   T   F

_____.

6. Hearn planned to return to America one day.   T   F

_____.

7. Japanese society was modernizing rapidly when Hearn was writing.   T   F

_____.

8. Hearn's children spoke two languages.   T   F

_____.

9. Hearn wrote with interest about the modernization of Japan.   T   F

_____.

C Find the meaning of the boldfaced words in the article from their context.

1. **Abandoning** probably means _____.

    a. bringing along   **b.** leaving behind   **c.** inviting

2. A **menial** job is probably _____.

    a. badly paid   **b.** interesting   **c.** well paid

3. **Dispute** probably means _____.

    a. contract   **b.** argument   **c.** discussion

4. **Immersed** probably means _____.

    a. avoided   **b.** got into   **c.** spent money

5. **Pivotal** probably means _____.

    a. important   **b.** peaceful   **c.** forgotten

A Number the sentences to put this biography of champion bicycle racer Lance Armstrong in the correct order. Two sentences do not belong in the biography because they are not relevant. Mark them with an *X*.

_____ a. The next year, he led the first American team ever to win the Tour de France, the world's biggest cycle race.

_____ b. Lance Armstrong is the most famous and successful bicycle racer the world has even known.

_____ c. His heart is so strong that it beats only thirty-two times per minute when he's resting.

_____ d. He was born in Texas on September 18, 1971.

_____ e. In succeeding years, his team went on to win the Tour de France seven successive times, a new world record.

_____ f. Just as his career was taking off, he was diagnosed in 1996 with a deadly form of cancer that had spread throughout his body.

_____ g. At the age of thirteen, he won the Iron Kids Triathlon, and he became a professional athlete at sixteen.

_____ h. In 1998, he returned to racing and won a number of important European races.

_____ i. He announced his retirement from racing in 2005, after his seventh victory.

_____ j. He decided to specialize in cycling, and began training with the U.S. Olympic team while he was still in high school.

_____ k. He speaks fluent French and can carry on a conversation in several European languages.

_____ l. After graduation, he began spending eight months every year competing in Europe.

_____ m. Only five months after treatment, he began training again.

_____ n. He now devotes his time to his family and to raising money for cancer research organizations.

B Read this information about Nobel Peace Prize winner Wangari Maathai and write a biography. Choose the most relevant and interesting facts. You do NOT need to use all of the information.

Full name: Wangari Muta Maathai

Founder: Green Belt Movement (1976)

Member of Kenyan Parliament: 2002–present

Number of trees planted: 30 million

Born: April 1, 1940

New organization: Jubilee 2000 Africa Campaign

Bachelor's degree: biological sciences, Mount St. Scholastica College, Kansas, United States

Doctorate: University of Nairobi, 1971

Winner: 2004 Nobel Peace Prize

Occupation: Professor of Veterinary Anatomy, University of Nairobi

Marital status: divorced

First woman in East Africa to earn a Ph.D.

Family: Three children (Waweru, Wanjira, and Muta)

Active in National Council of Women of Kenya, 1976–87

Purpose of Green Belt Movement: to plant trees and preserve the environment

Countries with local Green Belt Movement: Tanzania, Uganda, Malawi, Lesotho, Ethiopia, Zimbabwe

Purpose of Jubilee 2000: to cancel the debts owed by the poorest countries

Birthplace: Nyeri, Kenya

Nickname: Mama Miti ("mother of trees")

Elected to Kenyan Parliament: 2002 (98% of votes)

Supports: democracy, human rights, and environmental conservation

1 VOCABULARY & EXPRESSIONS

A Match these words with their definitions.

1. be inundated with _____   a. improve the quality of

2. slip your mind _____   b. period of time when you fail to do something

3. absentminded _____   c. make use of

4. chronicle _____   d. often forgetting things

5. arbitrary _____   e. be unable to think of a familiar name or word

6. association _____   f. decided without a reason or plan

7. lapse _____   g. connection, link

8. draw a blank _____   h. forget

9. utilize _____   i. have so much of something that you can't cope with it

10. enhance _____   j. make a detailed written record of

B Write answers that are true for you, using the underlined verbs.

1. What do you <u>remember</u> from your earliest childhood? _____

   _____

   _____ .

2. What do enjoy <u>reminiscing</u> about? _____

   _____

   _____ .

3. What are you <u>contemplating</u> doing in the future? _____

   _____

   _____ .

4. When you need to <u>concentrate</u> on studying, where do you go? _____

   _____

   _____ .

5. What do you do to <u>remind</u> yourself about an important appointment? _____

   _____ .

6. Can you <u>imagine</u> what you'll be doing three years from now? _____

   _____ .

7. What can you <u>recall</u> doing last Saturday? _____

   _____ .

A Put the verb in the correct passive tense.

1. An agreement about resettling the refugees (discuss) _____ at the United Nations this week.

2. Nepal, a small and mountainous country, (locate) _____ in the Himalayas.

3. A number of homes (destroy) _____ in a devastating fire last night.

4. Applicants for this job (require) _____ to have a degree in accounting.

5. English (teach) _____ in the schools of this country for twenty years.

6. In many East Asian countries, rice (eat) _____ at three meals daily.

7. It (believe) _____ that the first Native Americans originally came from Asia.

8. When the reporter arrived at the scene of the accident, the victims (treat) _____ by paramedics.

B Find and correct one mistake in each sentence.

1. The Pyramids in Egypt were ~~build~~ *built* without the use of machinery.

2. The leader of the criminals have been arrested by the police.

3. Electric cars are being sell in several countries now.

4. The peace treaty signed by the presidents of both countries in a ceremony.

5. Questions have asked about how the government is spending the money.

6. The winner of the contest will announced on September 1.

7. The exam papers have all be checked by two teachers.

C Circle the agent in each sentence. If it is not necessary, rewrite the sentence without it.

1. My wallet was stolen (by someone) when I was taking the subway to work.
   My wallet was stolen when I was taking the subway to work.

2. Some of the world's best coffee is grown in Brazil by farmers. _____
   _____.

3. "A Midsummer Night's Dream" was written by William Shakespeare. _____
   _____.

4. That sculpture was carved by a sculptor from a single huge block of stone. _____
   _____.

5. I was surprised to hear that the paintings were made by children. _____
   _____.

6. The heart transplant operation was performed by a surgeon at Metropolis Hospital. _____
   _____.

Who Are You?

| *Lesson B* | Personality plus |

1 READING

A Read this article with advice on how to study.

Remember This! Brain Research Shows More Effective Ways to Study

In many countries around the world, students of all ages are going back to school this month. Virtually every one of them has probably resolved to work harder, learn more, and get better grades this year. Scientists say the key to better learning is in understanding how our memory works. Recent advances in brain research are pointing to smarter ways to study.

Have you ever had the experience of looking up a telephone number and dialing it—then finding you've forgotten it five minutes later? That's because memory actually has three components. Sensory memory takes in the impressions from our five senses and lasts just seconds, such as an image of a street lamp on the eye that disappears quickly. Short-term memory works like a "holding area" for new information—that's where you keep a new phone number long enough to dial it. But, in order to remember that same phone number next week, it needs to enter into long-term memory—the area that contains everything from the multiplication tables to the name of your cousin's husband. Whether you're a first grader or a college senior, the purpose of studying is to get new concepts and information stored into your long-term memory.

Learning actually changes the physical structure of our brains. According to Dr. Carolyn Hopper, author of *Practicing College Study Skills*, every time we learn something new, our brains build new nerve connections with what we already know. The more connections it builds, the easier it is to remember what we have learned. "When learning something new and difficult," she says, "we need to ask, 'What is this like that I already know?'"

Dr. Hopper says that brain research has found four key factors in effective study. The first is making an effort. Our brain remembers better when we are interested in the subject, already know a little about it, and intend to remember the information.

Next, we need to find the most important points and concentrate on organizing them rather than trying to take in every last detail. There's a limit to how much information we can learn at one time. In reading a textbook, look for titles, headings, and illustrations that give clues to the main ideas. In class, pay special attention to things written on the board or printed in handouts. Try to imagine what you would put on the test if you were the teacher. Make up your own way to organize the important information, such as a chart or a **mnemonic** saying.

Then we need to reinforce the new connections in the brain. There are several effective methods for doing this. One is to recite the ideas out loud in your own words—"probably the most powerful tool you have to transfer information from short-term to long-term memory," says Dr. Hopper. For instance, you can try to **paraphrase** what you've just learned for a study partner. Another method is making a picture (in your mind or on paper) of the material to activate a completely different part of the brain.

Finally, we need to give the new material time to soak in—the new physical connections inside the brain have to be built up. For this reason, it's better to study in several short sessions than one long one. Avoid **cramming** the night before a big test, a practice that seldom helps.

"These memory principles work for any age group," says Dr. Hopper. "Being able to explain something in your own words is important, and being able to teach it to someone else is a sure way to assure understanding. When we read something, we are able to remember 10 percent, but when we teach something, we retain 95 percent."

By working with the way the brain processes information, students can increase their understanding of new information and retain it better. Mastering these smart ways to study will almost certainly pay off in better grades.

B Complete this outline with information from the article.

I. Introduction

    A. Memory is the key to learning

    B. Brain research shows how memory works

II. Different types of memory and their function

    A. _____

    B. _____

    C. _____

III. _____

    A. Make an effort

        1. be interested in the subject

        2. _____

        3. _____

    B. _____

        1. _____

        2. pay attention to the board and handouts

        3. _____

        4. organize important information

    C. _____

        1. recite out loud

        2. _____

    D. Give the new material time

        1. _____

        2. _____

IV. Conclusion

    A. Most important points

        1. _____

        2. teaching someone helps you remember 95 percent

    B. Using this information will help students earn better grades

C Try to write a definition for the boldfaced words by looking at their context.

1. **Cramming** probably means _____

2. **Paraphrase** probably means _____

3. **Mnemonic** probably means _____

2 WRITING

A Circle the type of mistake in each sentence: *C* for *comma splice*, *F* for *fragment*, or *R* for *run-on sentence.* Then rewrite it correctly, adding whatever is needed.

1. Only children are comfortable around adults they are friendly and outgoing. C F R

_____ .

2. The new software is hard to install, it's also difficult to use. C F R

_____ .

3. My older brother, who is ten years older than me. C F R

_____ .

4. Please answer all the questions you should not write your name on the paper. C F R

_____ .

5. Oldest children are dependable, middle kids like to be peacekeepers. C F R

_____ .

6. Would you like to meet in my office should we use the conference room? C F R

_____ .

7. After living for more than twenty years in New York City. C F R

_____ .

8. You should eat fruit containing Vitamin C every day oranges contain the most. C F R

_____ .

B You are going to write an essay about the personalities of two of your friends. Choose two people and write notes describing them.

Name: _____   Name: _____

_____   _____

_____   _____

_____   _____

_____   _____

_____   _____

_____   _____

_____   _____

_____   _____

_____   _____

C Write an essay about your two friends and how they are similar and different.

Par. 1: Introduction—Who are your two friends? How do you know them?

Par. 2: How your two friends are similar

Par. 3: How your two friends are different

Par. 4: Conclusion—Why are these two friends important to you?

Useful expressions
For similarities: *One similarity is . . . /Both of my friends . . . /One thing my friends have in common is . . .*
For differences: *One important difference is . . . /In contrast . . . /On the other hand . . .*

_____
_____
_____
_____
_____
_____
_____
_____
_____
_____
_____
_____
_____
_____
_____
_____
_____
_____
_____
_____
_____
_____
_____
_____
_____
_____
_____
_____
_____
_____
_____
_____
_____
_____
_____
_____
_____
_____
_____
_____
_____

1 VOCABULARY & EXPRESSIONS

A Complete the sentences with a word or expression from the box, making all necessary changes.

misgivings	warm up to	absurd	keep on
win over	think on your feet	linear	simultaneously
keep up with	mindless	lose track	

1. I'm going to _____ exercising every day before breakfast, even during my vacation. I promised myself I wouldn't stop.

2. My desk phone and my cell phone both rang _____. I didn't know which one to answer first!

3. My mother didn't want me to go overseas to study next year, but now she's slowly _____ the idea.

4. For me, playing computer games is a completely _____ activity. I don't even think about what I'm doing.

5. Emily _____ at least ten different soap operas on TV. She doesn't want to miss even a single day!

6. I think it's _____ to give teenagers credit cards. It's ridiculous to let them spend as much money as they want.

7. Cecilia has _____ about her new English class. She's afraid that the level will be too advanced for her.

8. Sorry I'm late! I was talking to my boyfriend on the phone and I completely _____ of the time.

9. It's easier to understand a movie when it has a simple, _____ story that just moves forward in time.

10. At first, my father didn't like my girlfriend, but gradually we were able to _____ him _____.

11. To be a successful businessperson, you need to be able to _____ and make quick decisions.

B Combine one word from each box to make a compound adjective with the given meaning.

light	long	pleasure	smooth	hearted	minded	seeking	skinned
labor	thick	absent		talking	saving	lasting	

1. happy and unworried _____

2. very persuasive _____

3. making work easier _____

4. forgetful _____

5. looking for fun _____

6. not sensitive _____

7. strong, durable _____

2 GRAMMAR

A Rewrite the underlined phrases using the correct form of a phrasal verb from the box. Separate the verb and particle if possible.

> show up   make up   clear up   give up   put away   go over
> face up to   move on   run into   dress up   do over   talk into

1. I hadn't seen Joe in years, and then I <u>met him by accident</u> at a concert last week. _____
_____.

2. When I go out dancing, I really love to <u>put on fancy clothes</u>. _____
_____.

3. My doctor told me that smoking would give me wrinkles, so I decided to <u>stop doing it</u>. _____
_____.

4. Tanisha broke up with her boyfriend last year, and she's still crying. I think it's time for her to <u>do something new</u>.
_____.

5. We waited an hour for Kyle to <u>arrive</u> at the restaurant. He's always late for everything. _____
_____.

6. I wanted to spend my vacation at home, but my wife <u>persuaded me</u> to go to New York. _____
_____.

7. After you finish using books in the library, you should <u>replace them</u> on the shelf yourself. _____
_____.

8. I had a terrible fight with my boyfriend on my birthday, but we <u>reconciled</u> the next day. _____
_____.

9. You must <u>accept</u> the fact that your grades aren't good enough to get a scholarship. _____
_____.

10. These accounts are full of mistakes! Please <u>rewrite them</u>. _____
_____.

11. The directions for using the copy machine are complicated. Would you like me to <u>repeat them</u> again? _____
_____.

12. I was having a lot of disagreements with my boss, but we were able to <u>resolve them</u> by having an honest
discussion. _____
_____.

B Write true answers to these questions, using the phrasal verbs in Activity A.

1. When did a friend convince you to do something you later regretted? _____
_____.

2. When do you like to put on fancy clothes? _____
_____.

3. Do you always arrive for appointments on time? _____
_____.

4. When did you meet someone you know in a very surprising place? _____
_____.

5. Have you ever stopped a bad habit? For how long? _____

Happy Days

| *Lesson B* | Look at the bright side! |

1 READING

A Read this article about the happiness of different countries.

World's Happiest Countries Ranked: Developing Countries Take Top and Bottom
by Denika Mitchell

If asked to associate happiness with a place, many people would picture the warm beaches of Jamaica with local children frolicking in the surf while Bob Marley's "One Love" plays in the background. Yet, according to a new survey by the United Kingdom's *New Scientist* magazine, this scene should be displaced a few thousand miles east, to the shores of Africa's most populous country, Nigeria.

In a study of over sixty-five countries conducted from 1999 to 2001, Nigeria was reported to have the highest percentage of happy people, right ahead of Mexico, Venezuela, El Salvador, and Puerto Rico.

Eastern European countries Russia, Armenia, and Romania were reported to have the lowest percentage. Economic and industrial giants, the United States and Great Britain, placed at sixteen and twenty-four, respectively. For some, this study proves the maxim "money cannot buy happiness."

Nigerian students at Howard University seem to agree. Freshman premed student Eron Oronsaye said, "Nigerian people are some of the happiest people I know simply because we have a strong cultural foundation. In Nigeria, it is more laid-back and family oriented—they hold deeper values than in the U.S."

Senior marketing major and this year's Mr. School of Business Ugi Ugwuomo added, "Nigerians are deeply rooted in tradition and family. You can see our values and culture all over the world, as we are the highest percentage of Africans both outside of Africa and on the continent. We tend to celebrate a lot of things; even in spite of problems, we have cause for some kind of celebration."

On the continent, Nigerians have had many reasons to be happy. At the time this survey was conducted, Nigeria had just made the transition from a

military-based government to civilian rule. Nigerian had also adopted a new constitution at this time, following sixteen years of government corruption.

Lately, though, Nigeria has been plagued by economic and cultural woes, with ethnic and religious clashes making international news lately. Yet, unlike many Americans, many Nigerians seem to view happiness as something that can be separated from the issues of the world around them.

Freshman biology major Olu Okeanawi explained, "Nigerians have been through so much that they can no longer let many issues faze them. As long as everything is fine within your family, you have no major problems. I think that it is our intense faith and spirituality that allow us not to feel trapped by material things and issues."

Freshman English major and American Kathryn Hurley feels that it is many Americans' materialism that controls their level of happiness. "So many people are so concerned with what kind of car they can drive and what designer their clothes are by," she said, "that they miss out on the simpler things in life that bring you happiness—family, friends, and love."

According to the survey, the factors that determine happiness fluctuate from country to country. As self-expression and success are the most important to Americans, satisfying one's duty to family and society is ranked highly by the Japanese.

Freshman Shemeia Whigham questioned the validity of the survey saying, "How can a survey tell how happy an entire country is? People have their good and bad days. No one is eternally happy."

While no one can be sure how factual this survey proves to be, feel free to test this theory out firsthand. Spring break is coming, tourism is encouraged, and a round-trip ticket to Nigeria starts at $1,054.

B Write the speaker's name by his/her opinion.

> Eron   Ugi   Olu   Kathryn   Shemeia

1. _____ thinks that the rankings produced by this research don't really tell how happy an individual person is.

2. _____ believes that people in developed countries place too much emphasis on possessions.

3. _____ says that happiness within the family is more important than what's happening in the outside world.

4. _____ believes that it's important to find things to be happy about, even in difficult times.

5. _____ thinks that a strong cultural foundation is an important factor in a country's happiness.

6. _____ believes Nigerians' intense faith and spirituality make them happy.

7. _____ is of the opinion that the level of happiness changes from day to day.

8. _____ feels that Nigerians hold deeper values than Americans.

9. _____ thinks that people in developed countries miss out on the simpler things.

10. _____ points out that Nigerians always have something to celebrate.

C Answer the questions.

1. Which of the speakers do you agree with most? Why? _____

_____

_____

2. Do you disagree with any of them? Why? _____

_____

_____

3. Is your country mentioned in the article? If so, do you agree with what the article says? If not, how do you think your country would rank on the "happiness scale"? _____

_____

_____

4. Which of the factors mentioned in the article do you think are important for your personal happiness?

_____

_____

_____

5. Which factors do you think are important for "national happiness"? _____

_____

_____

A Read this personal letter and number the paragraphs to put them in the correct order.

October 16

Dear Lin,

_____ I had a great time with my brother. He lives right in the middle of Hong Kong, on a very noisy street with some great restaurants. We went out twice for seafood. I always thought Hong King was crowded and urban, but one day we took a ferry to Lantau Island and spent the whole day hiking. We visited a temple with a giant Buddha statue. Another day, we went to a great beach called Shek O. All in all, it was really relaxing, but I'm glad to be back home.

_____ Well, that's all the news from here. Say "Hi" to your family from me, and write back when you have a minute.

_____ Since I came back, we've gotten a new family member—one with four legs! Late one night, I saw a little brown and white dog with no collar in front of our house. He was really friendly, so I let him in and gave him something to eat. I asked all around the neighborhood, but no one had lost a dog. So that's how Snoopy came to live with us. I've read that people with pets are happier than people who don't have them—we'll see! He's a lot of fun, but I'm not so sure that walking him at 6:30 every morning makes me really happy . . .

_____ It was great to hear from you. Your letter was waiting for me when I got home from visiting my brother. I'm sorry it's taken so long for me to write back!

_____ Besides walking Snoopy, I'm getting plenty of other exercise. I also have soccer practice four times a week now. This year's first game is on Saturday. We won just two games last year, so things can only get better—right? Wish me luck!

Take care!
Robin

B Write an informal letter to your pen pal in Australia, using the correct format with five short paragraphs.

Par. 1: Thank your friend for his/her last letter

Par. 2: Explain what you've been busy doing lately

Par. 3: Write about something interesting you did recently

Par. 4: Write about something you're planning to do in the near future

Par. 5: Close your letter.

Lesson A | Fashion sense

1 VOCABULARY & EXPRESSIONS

A Read the article and fill in the spaces. Use each term only once.

~~pair (v.)~~	go together	go for	flatter	come across	project	image
instinct	pick out	coordinate (v.)	change out of	laid-back	stand out	

We asked our readers, "What's your everyday style?"

Sara: I like to **(1)** _____pair_____ an antique blouse with a pair of jeans, or a lace skirt and a leather jacket. Some people say they don't **(2)** _____, but I think you can **(3)** _____ various pieces of clothing if you have an **(4)** _____ for it.

Kayla: I hate my school uniform! I **(5)** _____ it the minute I get home. My mother still **(6)** _____ a lot of my clothes, but I just got a part-time job so pretty soon I'll have the money to choose my own **(7)** _____.

Jason: I usually wear dark colors and traditional styles because I think they **(8)** _____ me. At my job at the bank, I have to **(9)** _____ as serious and responsible, and clothes like that help to **(10)** _____ that image.

Eduardo: I guess I'm the **(11)** _____ type who doesn't like to worry about clothes. I **(12)** _____ whatever is simple—a t-shirt and jeans, maybe a sweater. I'll never **(13)** _____ in a crowd, but I'm always comfortable!

B Answer the questions.

1. What kind of image do you try to project? _____
   _____.

2. Which colors do you think flatter you? _____
   _____.

3. Who picks out your clothes? Why? _____
   _____.

4. Do you think you have a good fashion instinct? Why, or why not? _____
   _____.

5. Do you like to stand out in a crowd? Why, or why not? _____
   _____.

C Match these expressions used in presentations.

1. What this _____   a. explain . . .
2. This shows _____   b. seen . . .
3. The significance _____ c. means is . . .
4. Next, we'll tell _____ d. you about . . .
5. Now I'll _____   e. that . . .
6. We have _____   f. of this is . . .

2 GRAMMAR

A Underline the relative pronoun in each sentence. Mark *S* if it is the *subject* of the relative clause or *O* if it is the *object* of the relative clause.

1. The bus that I take to work every day is always crowded. _____

2. I have two friends who are studying overseas now. _____

3. Jennifer, who works in a department store, has an incredible wardrobe. _____

4. I finally met the woman who my brother wants to marry. _____

5. The committee that planned the party was made up of six people. _____

6. *War of the Worlds,* which I've seen five times, is a great movie. _____

B Circle the relative pronouns that can correctly complete the sentence. More than one answer may be correct.

1. I know a guy (who / that / which) won a lot of money in the lottery twice.

2. Becky, (who / that / which) lives next door to me, is a flight attendant.

3. The man (who / that / which) robbed the bank said he had a gun in his bag.

4. Tennis, (who / that / which) is my favorite sport, isn't hard to learn.

5. I always like the clothes (who / that / which) my girlfriend picks out for me.

6. My friend has a dog (who / that / which) loves to eat spaghetti.

C Combine each pair of sentences by using a relative clause.

1. I read a great book. The book was written by a sixteen-year-old girl. (that)

   _____.

2. Ed has new neighbors. Ed hasn't seen the neighbors yet. (who)

   _____.

3. We had lunch at the sushi restaurant. You told us about the restaurant. (that)

   _____.

4. Nelson Mandela is a great statesman. Everyone admires Nelson Mandela. (whom)

   _____.

5. Young-mi is a teacher. Young-mi works with small children. (who)

   _____.

6. I'm going to listen to all the CDs. I borrowed the CDs from my brother. (that)

   _____.

D Answer the questions using a relative clause with the given pronoun.

1. What kind of clothes do you like to wear for special occasions? (that)

   _____.

2. What kind of people do you like to spend time with? (who)

   _____.

3. What kind of places to you like to go on vacation? (which)

   _____.

Looking Good!

| Lesson B | Cosmetic procedures |

1 READING

A Read this interview on the subject of hairstyles.

The History of Hairdressing

An interview with anthropologist Sandra Hubley, author of the new book *Hair Today, Gone Tomorrow: A Cultural History of Hairdressing.*

Q: The celebrity gossip columns recently carried a story about a well-known actor cutting his hair short after rumors spread that he had cheated on his wife. What's the symbolism behind that?

A: Short hair as a sign of sorrow or penitence has a long history, actually. In a lot of cultures, having very short hair—or even a shaved head—is supposed to show that you're thinking about spiritual matters, not about vanity. In fact, a lot of religions have practices involving hair. We're all familiar with the way Muslim women cover their hair with a scarf. In fact, Orthodox Jewish women do this as well after they marry, and Catholic nuns used to wear a veil to show their vocation—many of them still do. And it's not just the women. In the Sikh religion, men never cut their hair, and they wrap it in a **turban**. The Rastafarians also grow their hair long for religious reasons. So, what you do with your hair obviously has very powerful significance.

Q: Some people never **alter** their hairstyle. For example, the Queen of England has worn her hair the same way since 1953! What does that mean?

A: For many people, that would be a sign of stability. When a public figure like a president or prime minister gets a new hairstyle, people tend to disapprove. They think it's a mark of vanity and that someone of that **stature** should have their mind on more important issues.

Q: Have you ever changed your hairstyle drastically?

A: When I was a child, I had long hair that I wore in two braids, but I never really thought about it because I had no control over it—it was what my mother wanted. Naturally, when I went away to college, the very first thing I did was to cut it short. Really short—about an inch long! It felt great. And it was obviously a way of taking charge of my life.

Q: In your book, you say that hair also has a political aspect.

A: That's right. Just look at the 1960s and 1970s. That was when men started growing long hair and beards and moustaches, all to show their rebellion against the establishment. In many cultures, there's the idea that the more hair you have the more powerful you are, the more space you take up. In European history, it was a sign of wealth to have a hairstyle so **ornate** that you couldn't take care of it yourself. Just look at the kings of France, like Louis XIV.

Q: So, how important is hair?

A: In Central Africa, where I did some of my research, if you want to make a magic amulet for good luck or to bring bad luck to your enemies, it has to contain a lock of your hair or it just plain won't work. You can't make magic without it!

Q: When we go to the hairdresser, is it a fashion statement or a political statement?

A: It's both. People are obviously very concerned about their appearance, about looking good. But they're also concerned about the image they project and who they identify with. It's interesting to note that hairstyles are really starting to cross cultures more and more. These days white women love to get hair extensions—something that African-American women have been doing for years. And we see lots of Asian women, and men too, dyeing their hair brown or red, even blond. I think in twenty years we're going to see an even more interesting cross-cultural mix.

B Which of these statements would Sandra Hubley agree with? Circle *A* for *agree* or *D* for *disagree.*

1. Having a complicated hairstyle was once a sign that you worked very hard.   A D

2. A person's hair is sometimes a visible sign of their religious beliefs.   A D

3. Only primitive cultures see hair as a symbol of power.   A D

4. People like it when politicians get a good-looking new hairstyle.   A D

5. Your hairstyle is a purely personal choice.   A D

6. Fancy hairstyles are a waste of time and money.   A D

7. Hair has different symbolism in different countries.   A D

8. People sometimes change their hairstyle to try to change their lives.   A D

C Find the meanings of these words from their context in the reading.

1. A **turban** is a kind of _____.

   a. hairstyle   b. head covering   c. hairdresser

2. If you **alter** something, you _____.

   a. change it   b. keep it the same   c. try to stop it

3. A person's **stature** is his or her _____.

   a. intelligence   b. appearance   c. importance

4. If something is **ornate**, it is _____.

   a. old-fashioned   b. complicated   c. powerful

D Do your culture and religion have any influence on the way you wear your hair? Why, or why not?

_____.

_____.

_____.

_____.

_____.

_____.

A Think about these questions and write your answers.

1. List as many brand names for clothes as you can. _____
_____
_____
_____.

Do you think your classmates listed more, fewer, or about the same number of brand names as you did? _____
_____.

2. When you go shopping for clothes, how much attention do you pay to brand names? Why?_____
_____
_____
_____.

3. How are brand-name fashions different from other clothes? _____
_____
_____
_____.

4. Why do people think brand names are important? _____
_____
_____
_____.

B You are going to write an essay about brand-name fashion and its effects. Make notes of possible ideas to use.-

Effects of Brand-Name Fashion

Positive Effects on Individual People	Positive Effects on the Economy and Society
Negative Effects on Individual People	Negative Effects on the Economy and Society

C **Plan and write your essay, using expressions from the box on page 110 of your Student Book. Follow this outline.**

Par. 1: Introduction—How conscious are people in your country of brand-name fashion? Explain using examples.

Par. 2: The effects of brand-name fashion on people

Par. 3: The effects of brand-name fashion on the economy and society

Par. 4: Conclusion—Overall, are these effects positive or negative? Why?

1 VOCABULARY & EXPRESSIONS

A Complete the sentences with a word or expression from the box, making all necessary changes.

the ultimate	customize	snatch up	in vogue	fuss
differentiate	class	flashy	settle for	knockoff
extravagant	somewhere in the neighborhood of			

1. Makers of brand-name fashion spend a lot of money on advertising to try to _____ their products from their competitors'.

2. I'm not sure how much a private airplane costs, but I think it's _____ a million dollars.

3. When I got my new computer, I _____ it for playing games by getting a better sound system and some special graphics programs.

4. I wanted to get a new car, but I really couldn't afford it, so in the end I _____ a used car that's only two years old.

5. Actors and pop stars are known for their _____ spending habits, and many of them end up broke.

6. I wanted to have a quiet birthday without any _____, but my girlfriend planned a surprise party for me.

7. Cowboy boots are really _____ this year–everyone is wearing them.

8. I was really angry. I paid a lot of money for that watch, and it turned out to be just a cheap _____ of a famous brand.

9. For me, a week on a tropical beach is _____ vacation. It's what I dream about!

10. Adding a swimming pool will give your house a touch of _____.

11. I don't like to wear a lot of gold jewelry. It's too _____ for my taste.

12. Customers in the music store ran to _____ the new CD as soon as the clerk put it out.

B Match these verbs with their meanings.

1. civilize _____
2. immunize _____
3. prioritize _____
4. trivialize _____
5. generalize _____
6. monopolize _____
7. stabilize _____
8. victimize _____
9. equalize _____
10. personalize _____
11. sterilize _____
12. visualize _____

a. change something for one individual
b. protect someone against a disease
c. treat someone badly
d. make a mental picture of something
e. make something steady or firm
f. take complete control of something
g. make something unimportant
h. talk about the overall situation
i. make two things the same size or amount
j. rank things in order of their importance
k. remove bacteria from something
l. make a society more advanced or developed

2 GRAMMAR

A Read each paragraph and fill in the articles: *a, an, the,* or *0* (for no article).

a. This is how to make (1) _____ omelet. You need (2) _____ eggs, (3) _____ milk, (4) _____ salt, (5) _____ little oil, and (6) _____ large frying pan. First, heat (7)_____ pan over medium heat. Break (8) _____ eggs into (9) _____ bowl, add (10) _____ little milk and salt, and beat with (11) _____ fork. When (12) _____ pan is hot, add (13) _____ oil and pour in (14) _____ egg mixture. Let (15) _____ omelet cook until it is solid. Fill (16) _____ center with (17) _____ cheese, (18) _____ mushrooms, or (19) _____ piece of ham. Then, fold (20) _____ omelet in half and slide it onto (21) _____ plate. Serve it with (22) _____ bread or (23) _____ toast.

b. Today, (1) _____ large hospitals have (2) _____ many different types of (3) _____ specialized doctors. For example, (4) _____ gastroenterologist is (5) _____ doctor who treats (6) _____ people suffering from problems with (7) _____ digestive organs Diseases of (8) _____ heart are treated by (9) _____ cardiologists, while (10) _____ endocrinologists treat problems with (11) _____ endocrine glands, which produce (12) _____ chemicals that control our bodies. These specialists work together as (13) _____ team to promote (14) _____ health.

B Match the sentence with the explanation for the use of the article.

1. something already mentioned _____
2. doesn't matter which one _____
3. one-of-a kind noun _____
4. plurals that are general _____
5. class of things in general _____
6. specific familiar noun _____
7. non-count or abstract nouns _____
8. first mention _____

a. The blue whale can be up to 30 meters long.
b. Children are noisy.
c. I got a new camera yesterday.
d. She's the woman I told you about.
e. Chocolate is my favorite food.
f. The sun is really hot today.
g. Please close the door.
h. Training a dog takes lots of patience.

C List these places in the correct box.

Himalayas   Mexico City   Seoul   Czech Republic   Mount Fuji   United Kingdom
Lake Victoria Jamaica   Philippines Easter Island   Amazon River
Pacific Ocean Solomon Islands Argentina   Andes Mountains   New Zealand

Place-names with *The*	Place-names with No Article

To Buy or not to Buy . . .

Lesson B | My possessions

1 READING

A Read this article about an extraordinary book of photographs.

Life in the Material World

One day about fifteen years ago, photojournalist Peter Menzel heard Madonna's song "Material Girl" and started thinking. The media have made us familiar with the lifestyles of wealthy celebrities like Madonna, but what about the rest of the world? That sparked an idea. During the International Year of the Family, Menzel decided to investigate the lives of ordinary people around the world. It grew into an enormous project. With the help of United Nations experts, he compiled profiles of the statistically average person of each country and then located a person who fit that profile. In all, sixteen photographers took part, spending a week living with each family and then photographing them with all of their possessions piled up in front of their homes. The results were published in a book called *Material World,* which gives intimate portraits of life in countries from Kuwait to Samoa to England. Here are four of the families profiled in the book

Mali: The Natomo Family
In the photograph, Soumana Natomo, age thirty-nine, sits on the roof of his home in the town of Kouakourou with his two wives and eight children. It's a typical home for this West African country, built of adobe with a small courtyard. Natomo looks very proud of the possessions spread around them: a couple of beds with mosquito nets, a row of cooking pots, utensils for grinding grain, and a few extra clothes. Parked in the corner is his prized possession: a bicycle. His is a typical family in Mali, where many men have more than one wife, and large numbers of children are common. Out of a population of twelve million, 64 percent of men and 84 percent of women are illiterate; there are 30,000 Internet users. This doesn't trouble Natomo since he doesn't have electricity.

Japan: The Ukita Family
Sayo Ukita is forty-three years old and a housewife, and she lives in Tokyo with her husband and two daughters. The younger one is in kindergarten, but the older one is nine, so Sayo is busy already taking her to cram school lessons and helping her study. Their two-story house in suburban Tokyo is very small, and very full. For the photograph, they piled up all their possessions in the street in front of their home: a towering stack of furniture, electronics, kitchen gadgets, clothes, shoes, and toys. The family is almost hidden by their belongings. There's even a plastic house for their dog. But despite all these modern conveniences, the thing that they treasure most is a small collection of antique ceramics.

India: The Yadev Family
Life isn't easy for Mashre Yadev, a twenty-five-year-old mother of four children in Uttar Pradesh. Her husband, Bachar, works fifty-six hours a week for very little money, and they often are short of food. She must carry water from an outdoor well and cook over a wood fire in a smoky kitchen. But her oldest children are going to school, and she believes their lives will be better. It was easy for them to move all their possessions out of their small, straw-roofed farmhouse: all they own is two large beds, three sacks of rice, and a few cooking utensils. In the photograph, her husband holds up their most cherished possession: a Hindu religious picture in a beautiful frame.

China: The Wu Family
Wu Ba Jin, age fifty-nine, shares a small house in rural Yunnan Province with his whole extended family: his wife, two sons, two daughters-in-law, and three grandchildren. They earn their living by raising fish in large ponds in front of their home. It's backbreaking work, but they've done well, and they're proud of the belongings they've lined up in front of the house for the photographer: furniture, numerous cooking pots, and extra clothes. They've displayed their most important possession in the middle of the boat they use to tend the fishponds—their very first TV set.

B Complete the chart with information from the article.

(1)	(2)	Wu Ba Jin	(3)
(4)	two wives, eight children	(5)	(6)
(7)	(8)	(9)	suburban Tokyo, Japan
small, straw-roofed farmhouse	(10)	(11)	(12)
(13)	(14)	(15)	a towering stack of furniture, electronics, kitchen gadgets, clothes, shoes, and toys
(16)	a bicycle	(17)	(18)

A Read each pair of phrases or sentences and mark them *F* for *formal* or *I* for *informal*.

1. **a.** Let me know about that as soon as you can, OK? _____

   b. Please let me know at your earliest convenience. _____

2. **a.** I'm writing with regard to your letter of last week. _____

   b. This is about the note you sent me last week. _____

3. **a.** I have some doubts about those statistics. _____

   b. You are completely wrong about those statistics. _____

4. **a.** Dear Ms. Park: _____

   b. Hey Catherine, _____

5. **a.** Do you have time to get together with me on Tuesday? _____

   b. Would you be available for a meeting next Tuesday? _____

6. **a.** Take care! _____

   b. Sincerely yours, _____

B Rewrite these sentences to make them appropriate for a formal letter to a newspaper.

1. I absolutely loved that article in yesterday's paper. _____

   _____.

2. Spending money to buy useless junk is really dumb. _____

   _____.

3. Your reporter doesn't know what he's talking about. _____

   _____.

4. The free concert in Metro Park last night was just awful. _____

   _____.

5. Why don't you ever write anything good about teenagers? _____

   _____.

6. Building a city skateboard park would be so awesome!_____

   _____.

7. The mayor of this city is a complete idiot. _____

   _____.

8. A lot of old folks are really bad drivers. _____

   _____.

9. Wow, your newspaper is getting way too expensive! _____

   _____.

10. Can't you stop filling your paper up with advertisements? _____

    _____.

C Imagine that the article on page 58, "Life in the Material World," appeared in a magazine that you read. Write a letter to the magazine's editor giving your reaction to the article. Use the correct format and suitable language.

1 VOCABULARY & EXPRESSIONS

A Fill in the spaces with your own ideas to form sentences that show the meanings of the underlined words.

1. Some _____ are made of <u>cast iron</u>.

2. In my family, we made a <u>mutual</u> decision to _____.

3. I once saw an old _____ being <u>dismantled</u>.

4. After I finished _____ I had to <u>take apart</u> _____.

5. _____ are usually <u>circular</u>.

6. _____, which is one of my favorite works of art, <u>creates the impression</u> of _____.

7. _____ is made of <u>stainless steel</u>.

8. Over time, _____ <u>ebbs and flows</u>.

9. In our English class, we've done _____ as a <u>collaborative</u> project.

10. I have a _____ that's really <u>intricate</u>.

11. _____ was an event that was <u>sponsored</u> by _____.

12. In my country, you can see a <u>gigantic</u> _____ called _____.

13. Some students _____ to <u>cover the cost</u> of their tuition and books.

14. _____ can be <u>oval-shaped</u>.

15. _____ is something that <u>fluctuates</u> all the time.

B Complete the sentences with a word from the box, making all necessary changes.

| disable | discomfort | disarm | unarmed |
| uncover | discover | uncomfortable | unable |

1. Don't sit in that chair—it's really _____. Take this one instead.

2. The label on this medicine says that it's for the pain and _____ of headaches, toothaches, and sore muscles.

3. We are _____ to answer your call now. Please wait for the next available operator.

4. X-rays were _____ in 1895 by Wilhelm Conrad Roentgen.

5. Bank employees thought the robber had a gun in his bag, but in fact he was _____.

6. The police arrived in time to catch the burglar and _____ him.

7. One of my coworkers is _____. She uses a wheelchair, but she has no problems carrying out her responsibilities.

8. Reporters for the newspaper _____ evidence of dangerous pollutants in the city's drinking water.

2 GRAMMAR

A Underline the parts of each sentence that can be fronted. Then rewrite the sentence, inverting if necessary.

1. I never thought I would be standing here in front of this audience.
   Never did I think I would be standing here in front of this audience.

2. I would not give up my little dog Fifi for all the money in the world. _____
   _____.

3. She works on her paintings after her children have gone to bed. _____
   _____.

4. I buy an English newspaper every day in order to build my vocabulary. _____
   _____.

5. The people of the village were so poor that they lived in tiny shacks. _____
   _____.

6. A giant white shark was silently swimming towards them. _____
   _____.

7. Katie goes running every day because she wants to stay in shape. _____
   _____.

8. You will not be allowed to enter late under any circumstances. _____
   _____.

9. I haven't cried so hard at a movie since I was a child. _____
   _____.

10. The rescuers entered the collapsing building with great caution. _____
    _____.

B Complete the sentences with your own ideas.

1. Never in my life _____.
2. So difficult was my _____ test _____.
3. Under no circumstances should people _____.
4. Waiting for us in the future _____.
5. So interesting _____ that _____.

C Rewrite these as cleft sentences with *what*, *where*, or *why*.

1. I wanted to say, "I love you." _____
   _____.

2. Jane lives in a tiny apartment. _____
   _____.

3. He rides his bicycle to save money on bus tickets. _____
   _____.

4. We need stronger laws against pollution. _____
   _____.

The Impact of Art

| *Lesson B* | Hidden stories |

1 READING

A Read this article about the work of a unique artist.

Art under Wraps

On October 27, 1991, a gigantic 488-pound yellow umbrella, 20 feet tall, was torn loose from its steel foundation in Tejon Pass, California, by a strong wind. The umbrella, one of 1,760 in the valley, flew into the air and crushed a woman who had come to admire an unusual work of art called "The Umbrellas: Joint Project for Japan and USA."

The project that attracted the unfortunate woman—and hundreds of thousands of other tourists—was a massive installation designed by an artist named Christo. He is famous around the world for his giant sculptures, which he often creates by wrapping landmarks like monuments and buildings in fabric.

Christo's "The Gates"

The artist was born Christo Javacheff in Bulgaria in 1935. He studied painting and sculpture in Sofia, and later moved to Paris, the center of Europe's art world. Christo's first "wrapped" works were common objects, actual paint cans and bottles wrapped in packing material and tied. His works soon grew more ambitious as he wrapped tables, road signs, motorcycles, and cars and then tied them with ropes until the everyday objects created the impression of mystery.

With the scale of his projects growing, he began designs to package a public building. His first large work came in 1962 when he put up his "Wall of Oil Drums," an "iron curtain" that blocked a Paris street. In 1969 in Sydney, Australia, he wrapped a mile of the Australian coast in a loosely woven white fabric. Both projects demanded extensive funding and engineering expertise. Both of these highly publicized examples of his work were temporary, attracting visitors for a few weeks and then disappearing.

In 1976, Christo created "Running Fence," a 24.5-mile fence wrapped in yellow plastic that dipped and curved over California hills till it plunged into the Pacific and disappeared. An art critic called it "breathtakingly beautiful." Christo's next project, in which he surrounded eleven islands in Miami's Biscayne Bay with sheets of pink plastic, came in 1983. Two years later, Christo completed wrapping the Pont Neuf, a bridge over the Seine River in Paris.

After the 1992 disaster of the umbrella project, Christo was attacked by other artists, but many ordinary people remained supportive. A women who lived near the California umbrellas said, "Everyone was having picnics under the umbrellas and walking around smiling. They would be extremely kind and courteous to each other. I think it brought out the best in them. We won't see anything like it again."

Christo's works have grown ever more ambitious. For more than twenty years, he begged German officials to let him drape the Reichstag, a historic government building in Berlin. They finally agreed in 1995. In seven days, 120 workers and 90 rock climbers hung one million square feet of silver fabric and tied it with ten miles of blue cord for a two-week exhibition that attracted millions of viewers.

The artist's most recent installation, called "The Gates," was completed in New York City's Central Park on February 12, 2005. When the park was designed, over 150 years ago, its designers had planned to include gates, but these were never completed. So, Christo set up 2,503 gates inside the park, each sixteen feet tall and varying in width from six to eighteen feet. The gates were made of saffron-colored cloth hung from a stainless steel framework, and over 600 paid employees worked to set them up. The installation stayed there for sixteen days before being dismantled and its materials recycled.

Some observers have criticized Christo for the temporary nature of his work, but he disagrees with them. Says the artist, "I think it takes much greater courage to create things to be gone than to create things that will remain."

B Circle *T* for *true*, *F* for *false*, or *NI* for *no information*.

1. All of Christo's projects involve wrapping things.   T F NI

2. People in California were very angry about the umbrella incident.   T F NI

3. Christo's goal is to make art for future generations to enjoy.   T F NI

4. Christo does all the work for his projects himself.   T F NII

5. Christo's installations are dismantled after a short time.   T F NI

6. Christo has made a work of art with a government building.   T F NI

7. Artists have mixed reactions to Christo's work.   T F NI

8. People in New York were unable to use the park during Christo's installation. T F NI

9. Christo's first wrapping project was a motorcycle.   T F NI

10. Some of Christo's works of art can be seen in museums.   T F NI

C Write numbers to put the events in the correct time order.

_____ a. Christo wrapped a group of islands in plastic.

_____ b. Other artists reacted negatively to Christo's latest work.

_____ c. A woman was killed by one of Christo's art works.

_____ d. Christo studied in Bulgaria.

_____ e. Christo put up 1,760 giant umbrellas in California.

_____ f. Christo covered a Berlin landmark in silver fabric.

_____ g. Christo began making sculptures by wrapping things.

_____ h. One of Christo's works of art stood in the middle of a street in Paris.

_____ i. Christo installed a major new work in New York City.

D Answer in your own words.

1. Christo covers the cost of his installations by selling books, photos, and other items. Do you think the government should support artists financially? Explain your answer. _____.

2. What do you think about Christo's "installations"? Are they really art? Explain your answer. _____.

3. After the unfortunate death of a woman during Christo's giant umbrella project, many people stopped supporting his work. Would you have stopped supporting him? Why or why not? _____.

A What are they asking? Match the type of information requested on an application form with the question.

1. age _____
2. gender _____
3. marital status _____
4. employer _____
5. citizenship _____
6. ZIP code _____
7. date of birth _____
8. educational institution _____
9. major _____
10. degree _____
11. emergency contact _____

a. Is your child a girl or a boy?
b. Who do you work for?
c. What's the postal code there?
d. When were you born?
e. Where did you go to school?
f. What's your nationality?
g. What did you study?
h. Who should we call if you get sick?
i. What level of education did you achieve?
j. Are you married?
k. How old are you?

B Complete the chart by filling in one of the categories from Activity A.

1. marital status	single, married, separated, divorced, widowed
2.	NorTel Corporation, Pacific Bank
3.	female, male
4.	40403, 573-220
5.	business, history, physics
6.	Mrs. Betty Chu, phone 367-9976
7.	Capitol High School, the University of Texas
8.	17, 54
9.	Chinese, American, Brazilian
10.	10/15/87, January 18, 1974
11.	B.A., Ph.D.

Writing an application essay
To plan an application essay, you need to consider the question carefully, and then think about how to use this question to present yourself in a positive way. In writing your essay, be truthful, but don't include any negative information about yourself. You want to give the reader a good impression of you.

C Imagine you are applying for an international exchange program for language students who want to spend a month traveling in an English-speaking country. Write the essay for your application.

Essay: Consider your hobbies, free-time activities, and other interests. Describe which of these activities has been most meaningful to you, and why (maximum 200 words).

12 Our Changing World

Lesson A | Looking to the future

1 VOCABULARY

A Complete the sentences with a word from the box, making all necessary changes.

> fluid   undermine   coexist   brick-and-mortar   facilitate   breadwinner
> plummet   breakthrough   profiling   resistant   trigger   epidemic

1. Online banking makes me nervous. I would rather do business with a real _____ bank, where I can talk to someone.

2. The Foreign Student Advisor works to _____ international students' adjustment to life in a new country.

3. Some insects become _____ to pesticides after a period of time.

4. The announcement that tuition costs would double _____ a protest by students at National University.

5. Government budget cuts are threatening to _____ the success of our nation's environmental programs.

6. Today, students' educational paths are more _____, with many people taking a gap year or changing majors before graduating.

7. In our country, the number of families with four or more children _____ in the past twenty years.

8. The AIDS _____ is the greatest health crisis facing the world today.

9. The discovery of nuclear energy was one of the greatest scientific _____ of the twentieth century.

10. Researchers want to develop a form of _____ that will help determine who is likely to get certain diseases.

11. After my father died, my mother got a job in an office and became the _____ in our family.

12. In the public schools, children from different backgrounds learn to _____ and work together happily.

B Write true sentences about your city or country. Follow the example.

   The price of housing in the central city is escalating.

1. _____ swelling.
2. _____ escalating.
3. _____ flourishing.
4. _____ plummeting.
5. _____ dwindling.
6. _____ shrinking.

2 GRAMMAR

A Use the future continuous, future perfect, or future perfect continuous to write predictions about these things.

1. in 20 years / we / take vacations in space

   <u>In twenty years, we will be taking vacations in space</u>.

2. in five years / scientists / develop a vaccination against AIDS _____

   _____.

3. very soon / people / drive electric cars _____

   _____.

4. by the end of the decade / we / videophones / for several years _____

   _____.

5. by the end of this century / we / use up all the petroleum on Earth _____

   _____.

6. In the year 2100 / most people / drive hydrogen-powered cars / for thirty years _____

   _____.

7. in a few years' time / people / use personal computers for thirty years _____

   _____.

8. within ten years / many countries / develop alternative energy sources _____

   _____.

B Correct one mistake in the underlined words of each sentence.

1. By the time Ann retires, she <u>will</u> <u>had</u> <u>been</u> <u>working</u> in that office for over thirty years.

2. When you come to visit, I <u>would</u> <u>have</u> <u>already</u> <u>finished</u> my last exam.

3. Next year Dan <u>will</u> <u>have been</u> <u>studying</u> at a university in Australia.

4. By the end of the day, she <u>will</u> <u>has</u> <u>answered</u> <u>more</u> than a hundred e-mails.

5. Twenty years <u>from now</u>, <u>the</u> climate <u>will have</u> <u>been changing</u> completely.

6. I <u>won't</u> <u>have</u> <u>save</u> enough money to buy a car by then, so <u>I'll</u> have to get a loan.

C Cross out the verb form that <u>doesn't</u> make a correct future sentence.

1. We (go / are going / will have been going) to New York next Friday.

2. Next year Yong-min (will study / will have been studying / will have studied) English for five years.

3. I (will take / may take / am taking) the train if I can get a discount ticket.

4. My sister (will graduate / will have graduated / graduates) from the university before I start there.

5. Johan hates his job, so I think he (will look / will be looking / will have been looking) for a new one.

6. If you forget to water your garden, all the plants (die / will die / are going to die).

Our Changing World

| *Lesson B* | Are we up to the challenge? |

1 READING

A Read this article about alternative energy sources.

Power for the Future

One of the most **pressing** problems facing the world today is ensuring future supplies of energy. Our economy and way of life are both heavily dependent on petroleum, which will become increasingly scarce and costly in the future as we turn to ever more remote deposits to meet our needs.

Two future sources of energy that show great promise are tidal power and solar power. These are renewable sources of energy, which are in limitless supply and have the potential to fuel our growth and development in the coming centuries.

Currently, about 25 percent of the world's electricity is produced by hydropower, which uses the energy of flowing water in rivers, collected by dams.

A solar-powered vehicle

Research is currently underway to harness the energy contained in ocean waves to create tidal power. In this form of power generation, seawater enters a "wave machine," forcing the air inside to the top of a chamber. When the water flows out again, it pulls the air back down. This motion produces enough energy to power an electric motor.

At the moment, such wave machines are still small and relatively inefficient. They are also too costly to be economically **feasible**. But further development is expected to make them larger and more efficient, and some experts believe they could one day supply between 25 percent and 30 percent of the world's energy needs.

Unlike tidal power, solar power is a more immediately usable source of energy. The sun pours more energy onto the Earth's surface in one hour than all of humanity consumes in one year. The question is how we put it to practical use. Three approaches now exist.

First, the sun's energy can be used directly. Many new buildings are designed with large windows that face south to collect the sun's heat. Some large buildings in North America and Scandinavia already meet 100 percent of their heating needs from the sun. Solar energy can also be used directly to heat water for **domestic** use, and solar water heaters are already a common feature of houses in Japan. Solar cookers have been produced for developing countries in an effort to conserve trees that are used for firewood. By concentrating the sun's energy with mirrors, they can produce temperatures high enough to bake bread or boil water.

A second approach is to collect and store solar energy for use when the sun is not shining through solar panels. These absorb energy and can **transmit** it to batteries, where it is stored as electricity. However, they are still relatively expensive and do not function efficiently on cloudy days. Solar panels are now commonly used on a small scale for such things as powering emergency telephone boxes along isolated highways. It is expected that as production increases, the price of solar panels will continue to fall, making them affordable for individual homeowners.

A third and more **remote** possibility is collecting solar energy in space. This would solve the difficulty of providing energy on cloudy days, though the cost would be quite high. Satellites orbiting the Earth would collect solar energy and then transmit it back to earth. A series of satellites surrounding the Earth would be able to supply power twenty-four hours a day.

Some of these ideas may sound like science fiction at the moment, but researchers around the world are **collaborating** to make them a reality. Clean, unlimited sources of energy are vital for our future, and our children's.

B Mark each description *T* for *tidal energy*, *S* for *solar energy*, or *B* for both.

1. effective only in certain kinds of weather _____

2. not commonly used because too expensive _____

3. amount available is unlimited _____

4. can be used in a very simple way _____

5. being researched right now _____

6. is not used for large projects _____

7. could be produced far from Earth _____

8. small systems for individual buildings _____

C Circle *T* for *true*, *F* for *false*, or *N* for *no information*.

1. Solar power is mainly used today in countries with hot, sunny climates.   T F N

2. In the future, satellites will use solar power to operate.   T F N

3. Twenty-five percent of our electricity now comes from tidal power.   T F N

4. Governments have not invested enough money in renewable energy.   T F N

5. The sun produces much more energy than we need.   T F N

6. Cost is a problem with some renewable sources of energy.   T F N

7. In the future, engineers want to develop much smaller wave machines.   T F N

8. Solar power can be used to heat both air and water.   T F N

9. Tidal power is produced only in very cold water.   T F N

10. Solar power is more widely used than tidal power today.   T F N

D Circle the correct word to complete each sentence.

1. If a problem is **pressing**, it is (urgent / very annoying).

2. If a project is **feasible**, it is (practical / impossible).

3. If technology is for **domestic** use, it is used in (factories / homes).

4. If you **transmit** something, you (send it / throw it away).

5. If something is **remote**, it's (close / far away).

6. If people **collaborate**, they (work together / compete).

A What will education be like twenty years from now? Make notes of your predictions for these things—both things that will change and things that will remain the same.

textbooks
years of required education
teachers
subjects studied
use of the Internet
classrooms
homework

B You are going to write an academic essay giving your ideas about future changes in education. Circle your opinions to form your thesis statement.

I believe there will be (many / several / a few) (minor / major) changes in education in the next twenty years.

C Plan your essay and then write it. Choose three areas from the chart in Activity A that you will use to support your thesis statement.

Par 1: Introduction—containing your thesis statement

Par 2: Ideas from the first area to support your thesis

Par 3: Ideas from the second area to support your thesis

Par 4: Ideas from the third area to support your thesis

Par 5: Conclusion—with your opinion about the effects of these changes